CATCHING
FIRE
BECOMING
FLAME

OTHER BOOKS AND MEDIA
BY ALBERT HAASE, OFM

ENKINDLED:
Holy Spirit, Holy Gifts,
coauthored with Bridget Haase, OSU

INSTRUMENTS OF CHRIST:
Reflections on the Peace Prayer of St. Francis of Assisi

COMING HOME TO YOUR TRUE SELF:
Leaving the Emptiness of False Attractions

LIVING THE LORD'S PRAYER:
The Way of the Disciple

THE LORD'S PRAYER:
A Summary of the Entire Gospel (Five CDs)

THIS SACRED MOMENT:
Becoming Holy Right Where You Are

THE LIFE OF ANTONY OF EGYPT
by Athanasius, A Paraphrase

ALBERT HAASE, OFM

CATCHING FIRE BECOMING FLAME

A GUIDE FOR SPIRITUAL TRANSFORMATION

PARACLETE PRESS
BREWSTER, MASSACHUSETTS

2013 First, Second, Third Printing

Catching Fire, Becoming Flame: A Guide for Spiritual Transformation

Copyright © 2013 by Albert Haase OFM

ISBN 978-1-61261-297-3

Unless otherwise noted, Scripture references are taken the New Revised Standard Version Bible: Catholic Edition copyright © 1993 and 1989 by the Division of Christian Education of the National Council of the Churches of Christ in the United States of America, and are used by permission. All rights reserved

Scripture references marked THE MESSAGE are taken from *The Message*. Copyright © 1993, 1994, 1995, 1996, 2000, 2001, 2002. Used by permission of NavPress Publishing Group.

Websites cited in this book were active and accessible as of November 30, 2012.

The Paraclete Press name and logo (dove on cross) are registered trademarks of Paraclete Press, Inc.

Library of Congress Cataloging-in-Publication Data:

Haase, Albert, 1955-
  Catching fire, becoming flame : a guide for spiritual transformation / Albert Haase, OFM.
    pages cm
  ISBN 978-1-61261-297-3 (trade pbk.)
  1. Spiritual life--Christianity. I. Title.
  BV4501.3.H324 2013
  243--dc23   2013000185

10 9 8 7 6 5 4 3

Published by Paraclete Press
Brewster, Massachusetts
www.paracletepress.com
Printed in the United States of America

Abba Lot went to see Abba Joseph and said to him, "Abba, as far as I can, I say my little office, I fast a little, I pray and meditate, I live in peace and as far as I can, I purify my thoughts. What else can I do?"

Then the old man stood up and stretched his hands toward heaven. His fingers became like ten lamps of fire and he said to him, "If you will, you can become all flame."

—The Sayings of the Desert Fathers

CONTENTS

FANNING THE FLAME   **117**
DISCERNMENT

BECOMING ALL FLAME   **157**
DYNAMIC COMMITMENTS

CONCLUSION
A PRAYER AT THE HEARTH OF THE HEART

GOD'S PASSION, OUR ENTHUSIASM

My friend Helen is the mother of two daughters. She's a retired executive assistant for a senior partner in a global financial services firm. She's a good wife, an honest woman, and a faithful friend. She's also dedicated to her faith and committed to working on her relationship with God. I nodded in agreement when I heard someone say, "You can feel her fire in everything Helen says and does."

Helen is an ordinary person who enjoys babysitting her grandchildren, raising African violets, and meandering down the grocery aisle looking for bargains. But in her enthusiasm, I think she's extraordinary. Her love for God moves her to pause and pray at the site of a beautiful sunset over the ocean—and drives her presence when volunteers are needed for the annual church cleaning. Her passion for the homeless fuels the care and concern she exudes as she pours an extra ladle of meat sauce on spaghetti at the local soup kitchen. Her gratitude glows in the many thank-you notes she deliberately handwrites every month to friends and neighbors.

Eight hundred years before Helen, Francis of Assisi was also consumed with a godly enthusiasm. His love for God burned so ardently that he became a living image of the crucified Christ, branded with the five wounds of the stigmata—something rarely experienced among us today. But, much like my friend Helen, he showed what happens when a person responds to God's longing for us.

Throughout history hundreds of thousands of people have known the fiery passion God has for being in a relationship with us. The sparks from God's longing catch fire in their lives, and by engaging and responding to it, ordinary people like Helen and Francis become beacons of light who blaze by day and shine brightly by night.

Catching Fire, Becoming Flame: A Guide for Spiritual Transformation gives you the practical tools and time-honored techniques to do the same. It shows you how to respond to God's fiery passion, how to engage it, and, most important, how to be changed by it. Each of its chapters is purposely short and concise, allowing you ample time in one convenient sitting not only to read it, but also to reflect on its questions or practice the presented technique.

Each chapter concludes with a "Go Deeper" section. That's where you'll find additional resources about the chapter's topic that I recommend based on my thirty years of experience as a spiritual director and student of Christian spirituality. These resources will deepen your appreciation and understanding of the specific topic.

This book is designed to be a handy resource for expanding your knowledge and practice of ancient and contemporary spiritual practices. It will fuel your creativity and appreciation for myriad ways to fall in love with God—which, in the end, is what being on fire is all about.

As you practice the spiritual methods of *Catching Fire, Becoming Flame* and make them your own in a distinct way, you will find the flames of godly enthusiasm leaping up in your own life as they do in the lives of all holy people. You will also find yourself gradually transformed into your truest identity: a little Christ—which is what the word *Christian* literally means—sent to respond lovingly to the unmet need or required duty of the present moment.

Albert Haase, OFM
Feast of Pentecost

THE
SPARK
FROM
GOD

AN INTRODUCTION TO THE SPIRITUAL LIFE

■

*God initiates the process of spiritual
transformation by throwing a divine spark into
our lives. God then waits for our response.*

CHAPTER 1

A PROCESS OF TRANSFORMATION

■

Sr. Elena is eighty-seven years old, blind, and spends her days in a wheelchair. I didn't notice her when I began preaching the week-long retreat at the retirement home where she resides. But on the afternoon of the second day, she asked someone to push her to me.

"Father, I have a secret to tell you," she said.

I leaned over and she whispered in my ear, "God l-o-n-g-s to turn you into a saint!" Her face lit up as she added, "If you respond to God's yearning, you'll be amazed at what happens."

A Lifelong Process

Though it's been more than a decade since I heard Sr. Elena's secret, I can still feel the ardor and passion that accompanied her revelation. In one short moment, Sr. Elena taught me that God's longing to be in a relationship with us spreads like wildfire in the hearts of people who respond to it. They can't contain what becomes like a fire in the belly, a burning in their bones (see Jeremiah 20:9). No wonder their devotion is memorable and contagious.

Let's take a broad, quick overview at the process God uses in preparing and then setting people on fire with divine love.

Catching and crackling with the fire of godly enthusiasm is a lifelong *process*. It starts with God throwing a divine spark on the tinder of the heart. I'll describe that spark in greater detail in the next chapter. For now, it's helpful to know that it often comes out of nowhere and can take many different shapes and sizes. It might be an attraction or religious sentiment that grips the heart. It might be an event or situation that stirs your devotion. It could even be a word spoken by a friend, colleague, or relative that gets underneath the skin and stings your conscience.

If we fan the spark to flame and then stoke its fire with spiritual practices, it will ever so gradually transform us into beacons of light for the world. Sometimes it might flare up, shooting its sparks elsewhere as it did with Sr. Elena.

Because this is a gradual, ongoing process, we have to resist the temptation to look for a single book, program, practice, or guru that will cause spontaneous combustion; there are none. How many times have I been tricked into thinking that by reading the most recent book by a favorite author or practicing the latest spiritual craze, I'll become a saint? Catching fire takes patience and perseverance; it's hard, fatiguing work. It also requires a daily commitment to nurturing and tending the fire once it's started.

As God tries to spark our hearts into flame and we actively respond with spiritual practices, we *are transformed*. Note the passive voice. The sixteenth-century Carmelite mystic John of the Cross compares this process of transformation to a log catching fire. The heat of the fire initially expels the log's moisture and other inconsistencies, blackens the wood as the fire burns on the log's exterior, and then gradually transforms the log into flame as it burns from within.[1] That's why we can look back some ten or fifteen years, reflect on our lives then and now, and ask with embarrassment, surprise, or disgust, "Who *was* the person who did *that*? How could *that* have been *me*?" This transformation occurs not only on the exterior and cosmetic level of our actions, but also, and more important, on the interior and cardiac level of our thoughts, feelings, and desires.

Living with a blazing fire does not happen on our own by sheer willpower. We have to rely upon *the Spirit of God* and divine grace working on us and in us. The Spirit, and the Spirit alone, is the flint for all holiness. The Spirit then also becomes the fuel for our enthusiasm. Without the Spirit, our spiritual lives as Christians flicker out and become cold; with the Spirit, we are sent forth as zealous torches of devotion.

A Little Christ

Catching fire is not supposed to be a flash in the pan. And it becomes just that if we do not spend time tending and stoking the fire set by God's spark. It will easily flame out if we do not commit daily, monthly, and yearly to myriad and varied spiritual practices that the Christian tradition offers and which are discussed in this book. Fire needs tending just as grace needs a response. There is no other way.

As someone responds to the Spirit's action, he or she is ever so gradually transformed into *a little Christ*, the very meaning of the word *Christian*. That's the essence of the spiritual life: we are called to become who we profess to be by virtue of our baptism.

The waters of Baptism along with their gift of the Holy Spirit fuel a spiritual transformation that requires a lifetime of surrender. This gradual transformation of our identity is not a mime act, a caricature, or playacting. Rather, as in John of the Cross's log metaphor, the fire of God's love purifies our egos; it ignites our minds, words, wills, and actions so that we can say with Jesus, "Not my will but yours be done" (see Luke 22:42). It is then over time that we reach spiritual maturity, "the full stature of Christ" (Ephesians 4:13). Like Christ, who came "to bring fire to the earth" (Luke 12:49), we challenge institutional religion's insensitivity to the outcast and marginalized by becoming arsonists of divine love and compassion.

For I was hungry and you gave me food, I was thirsty and you gave me something to drink, I was a stranger and you welcomed me, I was naked and you gave me clothing, I was sick and you took care of me, I was in prison and you visited me.

Matthew 25:35–36

As we respond and slowly grow in our baptismal identity as little Christs, our hearts expand and the Spirit enlarges the circle of our relationships. Our fire cannot be restrained or suppressed in the hermetically sealed container of a single life for the sole purpose of our own personal sanctification. "No one after lighting a lamp puts it under the bushel basket" (Matthew 5:15). That would indeed quench the flame. Rather, through the daily discipline of prayer, the weekly practice of sharing our time, treasures, and talents with others along with attending church services, and the monthly commitment to spiritual practices such as Scripture reading and journaling combined with a yearly retreat, our godly enthusiasm becomes like a wildfire, moving us beyond ourselves, focusing our Christlike lives on others, for others, and with others. It leads us right into the heart of a suffering, needy world where we are *sent to respond lovingly to the unmet need or required duty of the present moment.* As we cook meals, change diapers, and commute back and forth to the office, discovering who we are and how it's possible to stay on fire for God, we become torchbearers of God's mercy to the hungry, the thirsty, the stranger, the sick, the naked, and the imprisoned. Without a sense of mission, godly enthusiasm fizzles into bogus piety.

I remember myself in my late teens and early twenties as a needy, selfish, egotistical young adult. I often used humor to control people and situations. I still recall attending a party in my sophomore year of college and spending the entire evening desperately trying to get people to laugh so I would be considered the life of the party. Some thirty-five years later, through the generosity of God's grace and a commitment to daily prayer and other spiritual practices, I am no longer obsessed with other people's affection and attention. I no longer use humor as a subtle form of manipulation. Something has changed inside of me, and my selfishness and need to control gave way to a decade of missionary service to Catholics in mainland China. I know from my own experience that from her darkness in the wheelchair, Sr. Elena illumined a great truth: you will be amazed at what gradually happens over a lifetime if you respond to God's longing.

God yearns to set us ablaze. As we open ourselves up to this divine love, we discover a fire being ignited and then glowing and sometimes raging in our lives. We experience *the process of being transformed by the Spirit of God into a little Christ sent to respond lovingly to the unmet need or required duty of the present moment.*[2] God's longing and call for this process to begin sometimes come in and through our deepest desires and attractions.

■ REFLECT

1. Fire is one image that captures the intensity of God's yearning to be in a relationship with us. What other images speak even more deeply to you?

2. As you reflect upon your past, how has God's abiding passion to be in a relationship with you expressed itself? What has been your response?

3. How are you responding to the hungry, the thirsty, the stranger, the sick, the naked, and the imprisoned in your neighborhood or the wider world community? How do they influence your spiritual life and transformation?

■ GO DEEPER

Albert Haase, OFM, *Instruments of Christ: Reflections on the Peace Prayer of St. Francis of Assisi* (Cincinnati, OH: St. Anthony Messenger Press, 2004).

M. Robert Mulholland Jr., *Invitation to a Journey: A Road Map for Spiritual Formation* (Downers Grove, IL: InterVarsity Press, 1993).

Francis Kelly Nemeck and Marie Therese Coombs, *The Spiritual Journey: Critical Thresholds and Stages of Adult Spiritual Genesis* (Collegeville, MN: Liturgical Press, 1986).

CHAPTER 2

DESIRE AND SPIRITUAL AWAKENING

■

About four times a year, I am the guest on *On Call with Wendy Wiese*, heard every afternoon on the Relevant Radio Network. Once, Stacey, from Austin, Texas, called into the show.

"Father, I'm a happy stay-at-home mom with two small children. Lately, though, I've been restless and feeling a strange attraction to prayer. But I must be honest: my husband and I are not regular churchgoers. So I'm wondering if I'm just imagining this. And my jobs as a mom and wife don't allow me the freedom to walk away and hide beyond the walls of a monastery. I'm calling to ask your advice. What am I supposed to do?"

I tried my best to show Stacey the special invitation she was being offered.

God's Passionate Invitation to Us

God is always trying to awaken a dormant soul and set it on fire with godly enthusiasm. Our deepest impulses and yearnings for the things of God can be God's way of throwing sparks at us. Religious interests, pious aspirations, and spiritual longings that seemingly come out of nowhere do, in fact, show we have captured divine attention and that God is now trying to capture ours. We desire God because God first desires us.

The mere awareness of being attracted to prayer or wanting to make God some part of daily life is the beginning of the process of being transformed. Before that awareness, we are like sleepwalkers. Life is a task-oriented game characterized by flatness, sluggishness, and, sometimes, lackluster monotony. Many are quite content to live this way. Stacey certainly was. She had spent her days with virtually the same routine: bathing the children, entertaining them with trips to the park and zoo, planning the evening meal, and, on weekends, occasionally going to church when it was convenient for her and her family. But now a spiritual spark is touching and scorching her heart. She is becoming restless. And without her even knowing it right now, her phone call for advice is the beginning of her response to God. Sooner or later we all discover that restlessness comes into our lives for a profound purpose: so that we may begin a relationship with God. This is the awakening.

The divine spark of the Holy Spirit—the flint and flame of godly enthusiasm—triggers the awakening. Without it, we would be rubbing two sticks together in the pouring rain.

Wake up from your sleep, Climb out of your coffins; Christ will show you the light!

(Ephesians 5:14, The Message)

God's spark can find us in any situation, circumstance, or event. Some experiences are powerfully positive: a weekend retreat, the birth of a child, an uplifting worship service, a heart-to-heart conversation with a trusted friend, someone's profession of love for us, or the sight of a beautiful sunset. Sometimes the catalyst is painful: a loved one's death, the diagnosis of a disease, the loss of a home in a natural disaster, or being laid off from work. In either case, this experience of grace is unique to each person and tailored to his or her season and situation. The circumstances are limitless, since nothing is impossible with God (see Luke 1:37).

Two of the most formative years of my life were spent when I was a boarder in a Franciscan high school seminary in Cincinnati. At the age of sixteen, while wanting to improve my handball game and hone my public speaking skills for a state speech contest, I began feeling an attraction and magnetic pull to the chapel for personal prayer. I tried my best to squelch those feelings because I didn't understand what they meant, and I certainly didn't want my classmates to think I was abandoning handball for a higher power. I remember going to see Fr. Murray and sheepishly asking about them. With a wisdom born from his own experience, he matter-of-factly replied, "That's God tugging at your heart and looking for some company. Why don't you oblige him sometimes?"

The awakening is God's invitation to a relationship. But it still requires our response. God will never force or put pressure upon us; with utmost respect for human free will, God can only invite us, encourage us, nudge us, and entice us. God tugs at the heart. And God does so through spiritual desires and longings that are placed deep within us. Stacey learned that in her own life. It's ultimately up to us to do something about them, to respond to God's generous bidding to be in a relationship with us.

Human Hesitations

If we choose not to respond or throw cold water on the kindling, God is forced to wait again and use another situation or event to spark us into flame.

Two misconceptions might keep us from responding to God's invitation. One resembles Stacey's initial insinuation that, not being a regular churchgoer, she was somehow unworthy, as if it was too late for her to connect with God.

It is never too late to begin fanning the flames. God's patience and generosity are magnanimous. That's why spiritual thoughts or feelings suddenly like flying sparks arise out of nowhere and keep recurring. They are indications of God's insistent determination to have a relationship with us. Jesus's parable of the workers in the vineyard (see Matthew 20:1–16) speaks to this. A landowner goes out at various hours and hires day laborers to work in his vineyard. At the end of the day, when the landowner pays them, the laborers who worked only an hour received the same per diem as those hired at the beginning of the day. Jesus does not say the late hires received a full day's pay because they worked hard and gave it their all but because the landowner is "generous" (see verse 15).

A significant lesson of that parable is that our time and God's patience never run out. The important thing is not *when* we begin to get serious about responding to God's invitation, but *that* we begin. It makes no difference whether you are sixteen years old as I was or in your forties as was the Carmelite mystic Teresa of Avila. And the moment we respond, we lose any apparent disadvantage that our tardiness, laziness, or lack of previous motivation might have imposed. A simple yes to God—no matter when it is spoken—fans the spark of godly enthusiasm and begins the process of our being transformed into a little Christ.

Stacey's phone call also suggested another misconception that might keep us from responding to God's invitation: the supposition that a relationship with God requires the abandonment of all spousal responsibilities, parental duties, and employment obligations. As Stacey put it, "And my jobs as a mom and wife don't allow me the freedom to walk away and hide beyond the walls of a monastery." Nothing could be further from the truth. The wonderful thing about God's invitation is that we can accept it right where we are. Throughout history people have done so as they went to school, raised a family, or went to the office to earn a paycheck. That's part of the contagion of godly enthusiasm and the paradox of catching fire and becoming flame: the extraordinary occurs right in the midst of the ordinary; the marvelous is found amid the mundane.

■ REFLECT

1. Reflect and pray over the famous words of St. Augustine: "You have made us for yourself, O Lord, and our hearts are restless until they rest in you." What does this say about the attractions and desires of your life? Which ones speak of God's invitation to you?
2. In what ways are you beginning to become awake? What are the circumstances? What is your immediate reaction to it?
3. How do tardiness, laziness, or a lack of interest make it difficult for you to notice the sparks God is sending your way?

■ GO DEEPER

John Eldredge, *Desire: The Journey We Must Take to Find the Life God Offers* (Nashville, TN: Thomas Nelson, 2007).

Philip Sheldrake, *Befriending Our Desires* (London, UK: Darton, Longman and Todd, 2001).

Connie Zweig, *The Holy Longing: The Hidden Power of Spiritual Yearning* (New York: Tarcher, 2003).

CHAPTER 3

THE THREE STAGES OF THE SPIRITUAL JOURNEY

∎

As I crisscross the country giving workshops on the spiritual life, I am often asked to give more details about the process of being transformed by the Spirit of God. How do I begin to respond to God's desire to have a relationship with me? What does the process of spiritual transformation look like? How do I know if it is happening to me? These are important questions, and our rich spiritual tradition not only answers them, but also offers some sage advice to people who want to burn with godly enthusiasm.

If you are willing to respond to God's invitation that comes through an awakening, you will suddenly find yourself walking along what's been called the threefold path or the threefold way. Rather than being distinct, discrete stages, these three transformative stages to the spiritual life are more like processes, movements, or actions that occur at various times and at various levels of our lives.

The Stage of Purgation

Once awakened and ready to respond, we are like a spark that needs help to become something greater. During this initial stage of transformation, called purgation, we arrange the kindling and wood by deliberately fostering attitudes and actions that reflect a person who is serious about catching fire. The tasks of this first stage are characterized by the acronym CPR: community, prayer, and repentance.

Now the whole group of those who believed were of one heart and soul, and no one claimed private ownership of any possessions, but everything they owned was held in common. With great power the apostles gave their testimony to the resurrection of the Lord Jesus, and great grace was upon them all. There was not a needy person among them, for as many as owned lands or houses sold them and brought the proceeds of what was sold. They laid it at the apostles' feet, and it was distributed to each as any had need.

(Acts 4:32–35)

Community: We begin by building bonds of support with a regular church community so that we are around other people who are similarly on fire—or at least smoldering! Jesus himself modeled the importance of community with the call of the twelve disciples; the early church lived out its ramifications in a practical way.

Spiritual transformation is not meant to be a solitary, individual affair; nor is it done in isolation from the world. It stretches the heart beyond the ego— "from me to thee," as a wise spiritual director once told me. Becoming a little Christ involves selfless love and service. This is learned within a community of flesh-and-blood believers who "wash each other's feet," learn to forgive each other, celebrate life events as sacramental moments, and welcome to their table the poor, the sinner, and the marginalized. Christianity without community is a caricature.

Prayer: CPR includes the commitment to daily prayer. What is critical is not *how* we pray, but *that* we pray for an amount of time appropriate for our commitments and schedules. For some, the most helpful form of prayer will be a conversation at the same time every day, when we convey to God our thoughts and feelings and then wait in silence for God to respond. That's what I did at age sixteen when I intentionally started praying for twenty minutes every day. This form of prayer can conveniently take place on the bus or a commuter train. Others might find more conducive to their temperament a simple and structured pattern, like repeating traditional prayers while using a rosary or repeating the Jesus Prayer ("Jesus, Son of David, have mercy on me, a sinner"). Still others might turn to Scripture. One of the first challenges in the process of spiritual transformation is discovering the prayer techniques that fan the flame and make us receptive to God's continual presence throughout the day. I encourage people initially to try different and varied prayer techniques, until they happen upon the ones that are comfortable and helpful for them.

Repentance: The final task of purgation's CPR is repentance, which involves purging ourselves of the deliberate sins that we nonchalantly commit; it is about removing the moisture that hinders us from catching fire. We choose to start moving out of the shadows and darkness where we have been content to live. We make an examination of conscience, take an inventory of our lives, and take conscious steps toward moral integration. The Christian values that we profess with our lips become the Christian values that we intentionally put into practice: forgiveness involves letting go of grudges; compassion includes deepening our sensitivity to the marginalized; kindness means dying to selfish desires. Repentance and conversion—from the Greek word *metanoia*, meaning "to turn around"—demand changing the orientation of our daily lives.

The Stage of Illumination

Over time, if we are faithful to CPR, we will perceive the Spirit of God working in our lives. That awareness—of the Spirit's interior work—is a typical indication of the second stage of the spiritual journey, illumination.

Unlike the stage of purgation, which can be seen exteriorly, this stage is internal and, as the name suggests, is characterized by light and enlightenment. As the Spirit's spark becomes a flame and then matures into a fire, we begin to see how Christian beliefs and values make sense. We take on an intuitive understanding and wisdom of the things of God. The commitments to community and prayer, once requiring the effort needed for any discipline, become more natural and are the ways by which we express our deepening enthusiasm and love for God.

Trustful surrender characterizes the illuminative stage, as Christians give themselves over to the action of the Holy Spirit. While the stage of purgation is active, the stage of illumination is more receptive; we allow something to be done to us. This receptive stance is strengthened by the emotional sense of being led by Someone bigger than our own egos. The purgative stage's guilt for past sin is now replaced by the illuminative stage's sorrow for having wasted so much time. Selfless acts become second nature as we are shaped, molded, and prodded along by the Spirit of God. In this second stage, God's grace is doing the majority of the work and action.

The Stage of Union

Fidelity to the CPR purgative practices and the trustful surrender characteristic of the illuminative stage gradually come to fruition in the third stage, called union. As awakening can be likened to a spark landing on ripe kindling, purgation to fanning the flame, and illumination to catching fire, union is likened to the experience of becoming a torch with a fire blazing from within. At this stage, we not only know but also experience union with God and God's will: so united are we to God that God's desires are our desires.

At this stage, in a vivid and obvious way, we do not simply *live* the Christian life but are in fact *being* and *acting* as little Christs. Here the fire is stoked with the wisdom of the Beatitudes, and we crackle with missional energy and passion for the loving service of others. Like Christ and with Christ, we feel alive and sent by God as a coworker for the kingdom (see Colossians 4:11).

This is certainly not to give the false impression that the threefold path is neatly and clearly delineated; it is not. The three stages or processes are fluid as divine grace works upon human nature. We could be experiencing all three stages at the same time: the memory could be experiencing an awakening, while the intellect and what it is thinking are in the illuminative stage and the will with its desires is working on purgative practices. This means we don't complete the homework of one stage and automatically graduate to the next stage. That's why I remind people that it is a misguided use of time to try and track where they are. The Spirit of God is ultimately in charge of the entire process, and divine grace is often more complicated and messy—and sometimes simpler—than delineating these three stages might suggest.

■ REFLECT

1. How are you living out the purgative practices of community, prayer, and repentance in your daily life right now? Which of the three needs greatest attention?

2. Where is the Holy Spirit currently working in your life? How might your actions and attitudes hinder the Spirit's guidance?

3. What is God's will and desire for you?

■ GO DEEPER

Benedict J. Groeschel, *Spiritual Passages: The Psychology of Spiritual Development* (New York: Crossroad, 1983).

Janet O. Hagberg and Robert A. Guelich, *The Critical Journey: Stages in the Life of Faith* (Salem, WI: Sheffield, 1995).

CHAPTER 4

IMPERFECTIONS VERSUS SINS

∎

James was stuck in discouragement and regret.

"Once again, my short fuse was just too short. I came home the other day tired from work. The kids wanted some attention and asked me to play with them. Instead of giving them five minutes of my time, which would have more than satisfied them, I just snapped. I raised my voice and told them I had been working all day and just needed some time to relax. This happens at least once or twice a month, and every time it does, I feel terrible afterward. I've been working so hard on my relationship with God and then something like this happens, and I realize I am a total failure. Where have I gone wrong?"

Listening to James, I leaned back in my chair and momentarily thought how we struggle with imperfections—and sin!

Imperfections and Weaknesses

All of us, like James, struggle with imperfections and weaknesses such as impatience and anger. Before we accept God's invitation to enter into a relationship, we instinctively give in to them in a variety of situations without much thought or reflection. But after we respond to the initial invitation and then become intentional about an ongoing relationship with God, something slowly changes in us.

We are now in a position to do something that, before, we never could have done as well: take an honest look at our imperfections and weaknesses. In what areas of life do we need God's grace and the light of Christ? Awareness is a powerful tool in the initial stage of spiritual transformation. Simply becoming aware of our ongoing struggles is the beginning of being set free from them. Awareness is not supposed to load us down with guilt; instead, it should bolster us by making us sensitive and vigilant, helping us to reconsider and short-circuit spontaneous reactions and bad habits. Coming to an awareness of a weakness as James did is always a step forward, not backward.

Imperfections, weaknesses, flaws, defects, failings, and short-comings are part and parcel of the human condition. No one is perfect; in some areas we all lack maturity. These areas are often hooked to real or perceived childhood deprivations. In an adult, childhood deficiencies, whether real or imagined, may become predilections, inclinations, fixations, preoccupations, compulsions, infatuations, and sometimes addictions.

Here are some examples: A man raised in a family that struggled financially may grow up to become a hoarder and be obsessive about money and possessions; he may also be prone to envy what others have. A girl raised in an abusive family might grow up always looking for ways to feel accepted and loved; she might become a compulsive shopper or develop a chemical addiction to ease the emotional pain of her childhood. A "middle child" who felt neglected in youth might become preoccupied with gaining people's attention and admiration.

Such knee-jerk reactions form the heart of our imperfections and weaknesses. We do not consciously or deliberately choose them. They gradually become bad habits or predictable, spontaneous reactions that disappoint our best selves. That's why awareness is the first critical step in overcoming them and being freed from them.

Such fixations and compulsions need to be admitted and brought into the light. Once we become aware of our preoccupations and compulsions, we look for the emotional "trigger": the childhood memory, feeling, event, or deficiency that it serves, caters to, and appeases. We need to disengage the trigger to short-circuit the fixation or addiction. Disengaging the trigger is no easy task, and we can rarely do so on our own.

Bringing this emotional trigger to prayer is a helpful start. Twelve-step support groups have a track record for helping people live with addictive personalities. Counseling or psychotherapy coupled with spiritual direction is also useful in deepening the awareness of the trigger as well as its effects upon us.

Don't allow guilt to gobble you up. Discouragement and shame over your imperfections and weaknesses waste a lot of emotional energy. They do not offer any positive consequences. Awareness of a personal weakness ideally leads to action, not simply to a begrudging apology or a deflated sense of being a failure.

The Difference between Impulse and Sin

Sin is something very different from these knee-jerk impulses or emotional triggers that we often act upon without reflection. Sin is a conscious and deliberate choice. It is a firm decision—a freely chosen act of the will—to be self-centered, thus dousing the fire of godly enthusiasm and interrupting the transformative process of becoming a little Christ.

Sometimes we consistently choose a certain sin, and it becomes a bad habit: think of someone who consistently makes a choice for alcohol, food, or shopping that backfires into a full-blown addiction. What started as a willful decision becomes over time a chain of slavery that is no longer freely chosen. That's why sins can be more dangerous than we sometimes think.

Deliberately chosen sinful actions are typically commentaries and variations on the seven deadly sins: pride, anger, envy, lust, gluttony, greed, and sloth. These seven deadly sins feed our overemotional investment in:

- self-concern (pride)
- self-image (pride, anger, envy)
- self-gratification (lust, gluttony)
- self-preservation (greed, sloth).

We can become so wrapped up in our achievements and accomplishments that we begin to think we are self-made individuals. We obsess over what people think of us and begin treating those who dislike us as enemies. Without hesitation, we allow our desires to rule and make decisions about how we should act. We make sure we never run out of food, possessions, and money. Paul refers to the actions associated with these self-centered concerns as the "works of the flesh" (see Galatians 5:19–21).

I also like to think of sin in terms of an acronym whose letters stand for those acts when the ego takes over control, assumes total supremacy, and "**e**ases **G**od **o**ut" of one's life. Our enthusiasm is then quickly replaced with a hunkered-down self-centeredness.

But there is more to sin than acts of commission. The ego also throws its weight around with sins of omission. Closely aligned to imperfections and weaknesses, these are deliberately chosen acts that ignore the opportunity to express what Paul calls the "fruit of the Spirit": love, joy, peace, patience, kindness, generosity, faithfulness, gentleness, and self-control (see Galatians 5:22–23). Banking the fire of godly enthusiasm is not just about stopping certain sinful actions; it is also about practicing certain virtuous actions. Acts of generosity shortchange greed; self-control puts gluttony on a diet; chastity gives lust a cold shower; patience tempers anger; humble service knocks pride off the pedestal; perseverance pulls sloth up from the couch; self-acceptance and trust in God's providence put an end to envy. Such virtuous acts challenge us to overcome the emotional fixation with self-concern, self-image, self-gratification, and self-preservation.

A man had a fig tree planted in his vineyard; and he came looking for fruit on it and found none. So he said to the gardener, "See here! For three years I have come looking for fruit on this fig tree, and still I find none. Cut it down! Why should it be wasting the soil?" He replied, "Sir, let it alone for one more year, until I dig around it and put manure on it. If it bears fruit next year, well and good; but if not, you can cut it down."

(Luke 13:6–9)

There is also a corporate dimension to sin. Some individuals create and promote systems, processes, attitudes, and mentalities that are antithetical to the most basic Christian principles. Obvious examples are unjust political regimes or racist organizations such as the Ku Klux Klan. Closer to home are companies that have unethical practices of hiring and promotion or firms that are dishonest and turn a blind eye to governmental laws and municipal regulations. To the extent that we participate in such organizations and do not actively work for their transformation, we are coconspirators, collaborators, and accomplices to corporate sin.

Though the four Gospels record a few passing incidents when Jesus uses the word *sin* (see Matthew 5:29; Mark 3:29 and its parallels; John 8:7; 8:34; 8:46; 16:9), they do not give us a clear understanding of what he means by the term. Six of Jesus's parables, however, suggest that he equates sin with a flat refusal to change and grow, to forgive and be compassionate.

Pause for a moment and ask yourself the following questions: How willing and flexible am I to change my attitudes and behaviors that I know in my heart go against the teachings of Jesus? How often do I let go of a grudge or hurt and embrace the person who betrayed me? When do I ignore the beggar on the street or retreat from those marginalized by the church and society?

Believe it or not, you have just examined your conscience based upon Jesus's understanding of sin found in his parables. The parables of the sower (Mark 4:3–8) and the barren fig tree (Luke 13:6–9) highlight the importance of being productive and bearing fruit; hence, they speak to the need to change attitudes and behaviors—and be transformed. The parable of the unforgiving servant (Matthew 18:23–35) reminds us of the need to forgive as we have been forgiven. The parables of the good Samaritan (Luke 10:30–37), the rich man and Lazarus (Luke 16:19–31), and the judgment of the nations (Matthew 25:31–46) all illustrate the importance of love, compassion, and a generous heart. These parables suggest that Jesus understands sin as a refusal to be transformed by God's fiery passion, a refusal to catch fire. It has less to do with the violation of a law.

Many people, unfortunately, narrowly define sin as simply breaking commandments and violating rules and regulations. As you can hopefully now see, Jesus understands it as a deeper, more fundamental stance and decision: an iron-willed, obstinate resistance to catching fire and fanning the flames of godly enthusiasm, a stubborn refusal to be transformed by grace into a little Christ.

■ REFLECT

1. What are your weaknesses and bad habits? What childhood memory, event, or experience might have given birth to each of them?
2. How does awareness of your weaknesses and imperfections affect your spiritual journey? How can you change your life in light of that awareness?
3. How does Jesus's understanding of sin challenge your own understanding of sin? What are your deliberately chosen sins?

■ GO DEEPER

Karl Menninger, *Whatever Became of Sin?* (New York: Bantam, 1988).

M. Scott Peck, *People of the Lie: The Hope for Healing Human Evil*, A Touchstone Book (New York: Simon and Schuster, 1983).

CHAPTER 5

BREAKING BAD HABITS

∎

Before we are spiritually awakened and begin fanning the flame of godly enthusiasm in our lives, we are like sleepwalkers. We go through life unaware of the many ways in which we subvert the transformative grace of the Spirit. However, once we begin walking the threefold path and get serious about CPR—connecting to a community, praying daily, and making a conscious effort to repent from deliberate sin—we quickly discover that our moral lives are a lot messier than we had ever imagined.

Still, saying no to deliberate sin can be a lot easier than breaking the bad habits in which many of us are entrenched. Our misuse of food, alcohol, gambling, sexual desires, and shopping, along with obsessions about violence, love, money, anger, work, or our appearance, often hinder our loving response to those in need. Many of these have become bad habits that need to be recognized, admitted, and broken.

Steps to Freedom

Breaking a bad habit is not an easy task. But it's not impossible. It begins with awareness—the conscious recognition and realization that we constantly react in the same unacceptable way to certain situations or thoughts.

Writing is definitely not my preferred medium of communication. I think of myself as a preacher, not a writer. So when I am working on a writing project, I allow my personality to change from an outgoing, affable person who is quick to belly laugh to an intense person, consumed with my thoughts and ideas, irritable, and a bit standoffish. I was never aware of this until a friend called to invite me out to dinner and said, "Bring the preacher—but please, leave the writer at home. I want to have a relaxing meal." Something clicked inside me as I suddenly became aware that writing was the trigger that sparked a personality change in me.

Once we realize we have a bad habit, it's wise to monitor ourselves. The following questions can be helpful: When am I most vulnerable to reacting with the unacceptable behavior? What situations or circumstances tempt me to act in a reactive way, without reflective consideration? This kind of awareness and monitoring can help sensitize us to the emotional trigger that provokes the behavior.

Once we know what our bad habits are and what triggers them, we need to ask if we really want to change them. To break a bad habit demands the focused, attentive energy of willpower. If we say we "should" change this behavior, we are still only at the awareness stage. If we say we "want" to change this behavior, we are probably ready to continue.

We often treat our bad habits as friends even though they bring out the worst in us. And sometimes they are the medication we self-prescribe to avoid some painful thought or its accompanying emotion. Ever notice how temptations toward compulsive activity such as overeating, binge drinking, inappropriate sexual activity, gambling, or shopping suddenly emerge when you find yourself in a stressful or emotionally charged situation? That awareness reveals your medication of choice. So we need to give ourselves time to grieve the loss of these ill-suited friends as we struggle with the feelings and emotions that we previously did not allow ourselves to fully experience.

Once we have adequately grieved the loss of the habit, we can actively, consciously, and deliberately change and replace the unacceptable behavior with another behavior. Experts tell us that the new behavior must be willfully chosen twenty-one *consecutive* times before a new habit is formed firmly in its place. Think about that for a moment, and how long that will take in your own life. In the case of a false start, where we choose the good behavior for only ten or fifteen times and then allow the unacceptable behavior to return, we need to start again from scratch, counting twenty-one consecutive decisions for the new behavior.

We will initially experience life in a different way as we actively short-circuit the trigger of the habit. Especially in the case of addictions, counseling or psychotherapy along with membership in a twelve-step support group can be helpful in dealing with our new lifestyle and behaviors.

The Mind of Christ

The fourth-century desert tradition of Christianity offers a helpful insight that augments this conscious change of behavior. The early desert fathers and mothers believed that what we think about plays an important role in our spiritual lives. Thoughts matter. Disreputable thoughts create desires that fuel the passions of the seven deadly sins, which often get played out in action.

Thoughts → Desires → Passions → Action

For example, we might think that some particular possession will make us happy. Our desire for it fuels our passion for getting it and keeping it. This can then play out in the sin of thievery or selfishness or greed. Or we might see a person whom we are attracted to. We begin to desire the person. And this can lead to the passion of lust, which can be acted upon in a variety of ways. Or let's say a person whom we struggle to get along with says an unkind word. We want to get revenge. This desire fuels the passion of anger, which could be expressed with a retaliatory word or action.

Finally, beloved, whatever is true, whatever is honorable, whatever is just, whatever is pure, whatever is pleasing, whatever is commendable, if there is any excellence and if there is anything worthy of praise, think about these things.

(Philippians 4:8)

The desert Christians encourage us to actually *replace* thoughts that could potentially lead to sinful behavior with *different* sorts of thoughts. This was certainly how Jesus himself taught: "You have heard that it was said, 'You shall love your neighbor and hate your enemy.' But I say to you, Love your enemies and pray for those who persecute you" (Mathew 5:43–44). A change of thinking can help lead to a change of behavior. That's how the desert tradition interprets Paul's injunction to dwell on certain thoughts (Philippians 4:8) and to be transformed "by the renewing of your minds" (Romans 12:2; see also Romans 8:6; Philippians 2:5); it can lead to having "the mind of Christ" (1 Corinthians 2:16). We will probably never know for sure what the mind of Christ fully contains, but between the desert

Christians and St. Paul, this is some pretty sure advice! Thoughts both affect and effect our actions.

This practice has helped me deal with my own harsh reactions toward others. Over the years I've discovered that I have judgmental attitudes rooted in the belief that life is a race and other people are competitors trying to get ahead of me. I used to do all I could to maintain my pace and my leading place in that race. Shifting the metaphor for life from a race to a family affair is slowly changing the way I look at people and respond to them. Competitors have now become my brothers and sisters whom I struggle to care for, love, and forgive.

In each of our lives, bad habits can be changed by following a simple process of becoming aware of, monitoring, grieving, and replacing the unacceptable behavior. Changing our thinking helps to strengthen a new behavior and facilitates the Spirit's transformative work in our lives.

■ REFLECT

1. How do your bad habits and unacceptable behaviors subvert the transformative work of the Spirit?

2. Ponder one of your inappropriate actions or sinful behaviors. Which passion—which one of the seven deadly sins—does it express? Which desire of yours does that passion fulfill? What's the originating thought that gave birth to the desire?

3. What specific thoughts will change your inappropriate action or sinful behavior pondered in reflection question 2? How will you remember these thoughts?

■ GO DEEPER

Gerald G. May, *Addiction and Grace: Love and Spirituality in the Healing of Addictions* (New York: HarperOne, 2007).

Karen Ravn, "Tips on breaking bad habits," http://www.latimes.com/features/health/la-he-breakinghabits6-2009apr06,0,2419265.story.

"Breaking Bad Habits: Why It's So Hard to Change," http://newsin health.nih.gov/issue/jan2012/feature1.

KINDLING

BASIC SPIRITUAL CONCEPTS

■

*Certain attitudes coupled with
an awareness of basic spiritual principles
provide excellent kindling for
the spark from God to catch flame in our lives.*

CHAPTER 6

DOES YOUR GOD LOVE YOU?

■

Born of practicing Jews, Jesus would have been raised as a pious Jew. He was taught the Torah and how to interpret it. He was also taught the "tradition of the elders" (see Matthew 15:2; Mark 7:13) that circumscribed the religious practice of his day and determined whether or not a person was in good standing with the God of Abraham, Isaac, and Jacob. Taught to love God with his whole heart, soul, strength, and mind, he would have also learned that one should preserve a reverential fear and distance from this God.

But somewhere along the line, a spark caught fire in Jesus.

The image of God as Abba—Father or Daddy—was the fire crackling in the soul of Jesus. Everything that Jesus taught and did radiated from it: his outreach to the marginalized, his table fellowship with sinners, and his parables about love, forgiveness, and generosity were all sparks shooting from his insight that God was an amazingly close and intimate Father.

A healthy image of God can focus our own godly enthusiasm. It provides excellent kindling not only for the transformative process of the Holy Spirit, but also for our loving response to those in need. Unhealthy images of God, on the other hand, typically elicit unhealthy behavior. To think of God as a dictator, warden, or traffic cop will keep us self-conscious and hiding in the bushes, cowering in fear. An image of God as an amorphous energy force will keep our relationship with God distant, uninspiring, and impersonal. Viewing God as Santa Claus makes us focus on our wants, and imagining God as a divine puppeteer keeps us hoping that the right strings are pulled. Each of these images of God fails to enkindle the fire that challenges us to loving service of our neighbors.

No saint better exemplifies the transformative power of one's image of God than Thérèse of Lisieux. Realizing that holiness, in the tradition of the great spiritual giants who had lived before her, was beyond her grasp, she began to practice her "way of spiritual childhood." She daily recognized her nothingness, confidently abandoned herself to God, and expected God to give her everything she needed, just as children expect everything from their parents. Despite her debilitating tuberculosis and the personality clashes inherent in her convent setting, this practice of enthusiastic trust challenged her to renounce all worry and live the carefree life of a child. She described her spirituality of spiritual childhood to one of the sisters like this: "It means not to attribute to ourselves the virtues we practice, not to believe that we are capable of anything, but to acknowledge that it is the good Lord who has placed that treasure in the hand of His little child that He may use it when He needs it, but it remains always God's own treasure. Finally, it means that we must not be discouraged by our faults, for children fall frequently."[3] Thérèse's image of God as a forgiving, loving, and generous father ignited the fires of godly enthusiasm in her short life; she died at age twenty-four.

Upbringing, Education, and Experience

How we think about God does not come out of nowhere. It is often handed to us by our childhood upbringing, education, and religious formation. A friend of mine, Peter, who is in his early thirties, still remembers hearing his mother's childhood threat, "Wait until your father comes home"—and that now raises his blood pressure as he prepares for the Sacrament of Reconciliation. I think I first experienced dread as I hid under the bedcovers the night after stealing a candy bar from a neighbor's kitchen; while a thunderstorm pounded the sky, all I could hear was the priest at the previous Sunday's Mass preaching about God the Father's punishment and wrath.

Some of us cannot relate to Jesus's image of God as Father. We might find it even distasteful or distressing. Rest assured, the image of God as Father is not the key that unlocks Jesus's insight into God. The key is what the image conveys: the reality of God's unconditional love, total acceptance, compassionate mercy, and unrelenting protection. For Jesus, fatherhood points to God's urgent longing to be in a relationship with us. So whatever image from your upbringing, education, and experience best conveys that reality—be it friend, lover, spouse, shepherd, father, or mother—is the perfect image for you to settle upon. The importance of a healthy image of God lies not in the metaphorical shape it takes but in the godly enthusiasm it evokes for a life of loving service.

Changing and Evolving

We develop a healthy image of God over time. The first image of God that I can remember goes back to the beginning of my teens: God was an all-knowing, all-powerful judge who had a stern but fair sense of justice. In my later teens and early twenties, the image evolved into a compassionate, merciful father who identified with my disappointments and struggles; in hindsight, this image probably emerged as a consequence of my father's suicide and the subsequent loss of a father's presence in my early adulthood. During my years of missionary activity in mainland China as I struggled with the isolation that foreigners often feel, God was an ever-present companion who loved me unconditionally and offered a tender shoulder of compassion when I needed it. Now as I approach sixty years of age, I think of God as the conductor of the symphony of my life who, much to my utter surprise, calls out of me a melody I never knew existed.

Don't worry when you find your image of God changing over the years. That's natural as we grow and mature. An image of God that has remained static for decades can suggest that we have stopped growing spiritually or that we have come to idolize a mere picture—because, in the end, that's all an image of God is, a picture, not the person. If we are pliable, the Spirit will transform our image of God as the Spirit transforms us into little Christs.

Inadequacy of an Image

As I followed Hurricane Katrina and watched it destroy my hometown of New Orleans, I couldn't help asking, how could God possibly permit this to happen? That very question is a subtle reminder that every image of God is incomplete, inferior, and inadequate. Like the seven blind men who each touched a different part of the elephant's body and then thought their particular description of the elephant was accurate, so too we think our images precisely and faithfully describe the reality of God. But they don't.

Some Scripture scholars suggest that this was the sin of the early Israelites in the desert (see Exodus 32:1–6). In their desire for a comprehensive image of the Lord, they fashioned a golden calf, proclaimed it as their liberating God, and worshiped it. This is idolatry. The literal translations of the Hebrew words translated as *idols* say it in a blunt way: "powerless ones," "pellets of dung," "shameful things." God cannot be contained by anything composed of human hands or the human mind.

Though there is always a temptation to fall in love with our image of God, it's important to remember that God is utter and profound mystery: incomprehensible, ineffable, unexplainable, indescribable, and unfathomable. I can't state this point any more succinctly than did St. Augustine: "If you understand it, it is not God."[4]

Not only are language, concepts, and images straitjackets when it comes to describing God, but also they can be deceptive. Yet without them, God becomes like a nebulous and amorphous cloud that doesn't spark godly enthusiasm—much less a desire to grow in the image of Christ. We need images of God more for the inspiration they incite and ignite in our lives than for the information, inadequate as it is, that they impart.

Be perfect, therefore, as your heavenly Father is perfect.

(Matthew 5:48)

Reading the New Testament, especially the Gospels, helps us to know, fall in love with, and imitate a God who:

- values us more than the birds and the lilies (Luke 12:22–31);
- is like a shepherd in search of one lost sheep (Luke 15:3–7);
- is like a vine-grower who prunes fruit-bearing branches to produce even more fruit (John 15:1–2);
- is a thrilled father who barrels down a dusty path to welcome a wayward son (Luke 15:11–32);

- is a gracious and generous heavenly father who makes the sun shine on the evil and the good and sends rain on the righteous and on the unrighteous (Matthew 5:45);
- is a diligent woman meticulously looking for a lost coin (Luke 15:8–10);
- is a divine almsgiver who provides true bread from heaven (John 6:32–33);
- is like a party-thrower who invites the marginalized to a sumptuous banquet (Luke 14:15–24);
- is like a compassionate king who forgives a slave's large debt (Matthew 18:23–35).

A healthy image of God, rooted in the teachings and ministry of Jesus, fuels our enthusiasm, openness, and trust in the transformation that the Spirit eagerly wants to initiate within us.

■ REFLECT

1. What is your current, most common, image of God? How does it foster or challenge you to loving service of your neighbor? How does it hinder you?
2. What does your current image of God say about your upbringing, education, and religious formation?
3. Have you ever experienced God as an unexplainable, ineffable mystery? What was your response to this experience?

■ GO DEEPER

Frank DeSiano, csp, and Kenneth Boyack, csp, *Discovering My Experience of God: Awareness and Witness* (Mahwah, NJ: Paulist Press, 1992).

Albert Haase, OFM, "The Importance of One's Image of God," http://www.youtube.com/watch?v=1LTs9t5YrDo.

Michael Manning, *Fifteen Faces of God: A Quest to Know God through the Parables of Jesus* (New York: Doubleday, 2010).

John Veltri, SJ, "Our Images of God Affect How We Relate to Prayer and Life," http://www.jesuits.ca/orientations/image.htm.

CHAPTER 7

PRINCIPLES OF PRAYER

∎

My grandmother was a pious widow in New Orleans. I still have memories of how every afternoon at 3:30, she would turn off the television and spend the next ninety minutes, as she put it, "saying my prayers." She would read most of them out of prayer books stacked on the small end table next to her lounge chair. She also kept a list of intentions for which she would pray.

I distinctly remember the day she confessed to me "the prayer of last resort." "Albert," she confided, "when Jesus turns a deaf ear to me, I never get upset. I simply take my statue of the Blessed Mother, wrap it in aluminum foil, put it in the freezer, and say, 'Jesus, your Mama is in the deep freeze, and she's not coming out until you answer my prayer!' And you know what?" she continued with a twinkle in her eye, "It usually works."

A Definition of Prayer

Gram's way of praying was unique, and yes, a bit eccentric. I am not recommending that we all pray like my dear grandmother. However, anyone serious about keeping their fire for God kindled must pray.

Prayer is one of the three CPR essentials (community, prayer, and repentance) that we intentionally adopt as we respond to God's awakening grace; it provides kindling for the spark from God. Over the course of my life, I've learned that my grandmother, at least as I perceive it, saw part of the prayer picture. But there is so much more to this practice than reading what others have prayed, saying prayers learned by rote, or twisting God's arm to respond to a request. Teresa of Avila, the sixteenth-century Carmelite reformer, mystic, and doctor of the Church, offers us the most fundamental definition of prayer when she refers to prayer as an intimate friendship, a frequent heart-to-heart conversation with him by whom we know ourselves to be loved.[5] Some important principles arise from this definition.

- *Prayer should make us prayerful.* Whatever we do when we pray—whether it's saying a rosary, reading the prayers of the saints, spending time in reflective silence, meditating on a Scripture passage, or expressing our worries and concerns to God—should make us more aware of the presence of God, who constantly surrounds us and never leaves us. People who pray typically experience God's presence while ironing, commuting to work, and walking to the dorm more often than people who don't.

- *We each have our own way to pray.* If prayer is supposed to make us sensitive to the God by whom we know ourselves to be loved, the God who has a burning desire to be in a relationship with us, then we will each have our own way to grow in that sensitivity. There is no one-size-fits-all method of prayer. One challenge during the way of purgation as we begin the spiritual journey is to become comfortable with our own intimate way of conversing with God. This is easier said than done. It usually takes time and some trial and error to find the method that works for us personally.

- *We pray from where we are and not from where we think we should be.* There is always a temptation to believe we should be further along in our prayer life, that we shouldn't get bogged down with concerns or worries about our practical, nitty-gritty lives. Consequently we ignore our feelings and often pray around them. In doing so we might try to work ourselves up into an emotional high or find an inner space, attempting to be someone we are not. In effect, we put on music and tap dance for Jesus.

Such an approach ignores the fundamental fact about prayer: it is a heart-to-heart conversation. This means we should pray *from* our feelings and not *around* them. If we are angry, we pray from our anger; if we are depressed, we pray from our sadness; if we are happy, we pray from our joy; if we are lonely, we pray from our loneliness. Indeed, as in any conversation with an intimate lover, we are challenged to be authentic and transparent with God. This is partly the reason why the tax collector went home "justified" after his prayer in the temple (see Luke 18:9–14). He prayed from the awareness of his sinfulness.

- *The prayers of petition and intercession are expressions of care, concern, and compassion; they are not ways to convince or coax a change of God's will.* Petition and intercession are often thought of as rain dances or ways to strong-arm God. "If I pray long enough and in the right way, I'll get what I want" is a typical attitude similar to my grandmother's.

  But prayers of petition and intercession are really ways to express the first element of CPR: community, our love and interest in the lives of others. They also show our trust in God's fiery passion to be in a relationship with us and in God's loving concern for us.

- *Frustration in prayer is a sign we are trying too hard.* Frustration is a good indicator that we are not really praying from where we are, that perhaps we are being less than honest in our conversation with God. It might also be a sign that we are actively resisting the transformative process initiated by the Spirit of God. In either case, we are trying too hard—to run away from our feelings or to resist God's grace.

As master of novices, the famed Trappist Thomas Merton was responsible for teaching young monks the fundamentals of the spiritual journey. One day, suspecting that a novice was trying too hard to pray, Merton advised him, "Brother, how does an apple ripen? It just sits in the sun."[6]

That's great advice for all of us when it comes to a heart-to-heart conversation with God. Prayer should free us up and unburden us. We come into the presence of God just as we are and allow this encounter to transform us—to "ripen" us just as the sun turns an apple from green to red.

Challenges in Prayer

• *Growth in prayer is growth in silence.* As in any other intimate friendship, the more time we spend in conversation with God, the less we have to say. We begin to spend more time listening. And listening often gives way to just being in the presence of him by whom we know ourselves to be loved.

St. John Vianney used to watch a peasant enter the local church to pray. Wondering what the peasant said to God, Vianney asked. The peasant's reply was simple: "I look at him, and he just looks at me."

Maturing prayer is about loving glances. It becomes more and more simple and silent. This is not a cold, empty silence but the ecstatic silence of lovers—filled with a history of infidelities, broken promises, forgiveness, unconditional love, and a voracious enthusiasm to continue the relationship.

If we don't know how or what to pray, it doesn't matter. [God's Spirit] does our praying in and for us, making prayer out of our wordless sighs, our aching groans.

(Romans 8:26, The Message)

- *Dryness in prayer is a sign that something is happening.* There is a common misconception that if prayer becomes dry, boring, dissatisfying, or meaningless, we are doing something wrong. Nothing could be further from the truth. Dryness is always an indication that our prayer techniques are flaming out as God takes over and teaches us new ways to communicate.

  When we are not getting anything out of prayer, it's important that we continue to remain faithful to it. Just showing up every day and going through the motions is a bold act of fidelity that is blessed by God.

- *The goal of prayer is not a mind free of distractions but a surrendered heart of love.* Every time I pray, I have distractions. My mind seems stoked with green wood that crackles, hisses, pops, and shoots sparks everywhere. My attention follows those sparks and I become discouraged as I struggle to rid myself of the distractions; to make matters worse, the very effort to rid myself of them becomes another distraction!

Distractions are not as bad as you might think; they can be great teachers in the spiritual life. They sometimes indicate what we are really passionate about and invested in. They might also point out areas where we tend to throw water on the kindling. In both cases, distractions can tell us exactly where we are and become the topics for our heart-to-heart conversation with him by whom we know ourselves to be loved.

The aim of prayer is not the attainment of some Zen-like, thought-less state of consciousness. Its fundamental aim is a heart-to-heart conversation in which we learn openness to the call and challenge of the Spirit to lovingly serve our neighbor. As little Christs, we pray the psalm that the letter to the Hebrews places on the lips of Christ, "See, God, I have come to do your will, O God" (Hebrews 10:7; Psalm 40:7–8).

My grandmother's practice of putting a statue in the freezer as a prayer of last resort was unquestionably strange, certainly superstitious, and maybe downright manipulative. But it also bespeaks an intimate friendship, a godly enthusiasm, and a good-natured humor that are at the root of any heart-to-heart conversation with a beloved.

■ REFLECT

1. In what ways does your current method of prayer match Teresa of Avila's description of prayer? In what ways does it not?

2. How do you deal with feelings and distractions in prayer? When have they become your teachers in the spiritual life?

3. When was the last time you felt frustrated or dry in prayer? Upon reflection, what was the cause? How did you handle the frustration or dryness?

▪GO DEEPER

Paul Brian Campbell, sj, "Distractions in Prayer," http://peopleforothers .loyolapress.com/2012/03/19/distractions-in-prayer/.

Richard J. Foster, *Prayer: Finding the Heart's True Home* (New York: HarperOne, 1992).

Ann and Barry Ulanov, *Primary Speech: A Psychology of Prayer* (Louisville, KY: Westminster John Knox Press, 1983).

Philip Zaleski and Carol Zaleski, *Prayer: A History* (New York: Mariner Books, 2006).

CHAPTER 8

THE ATTITUDE OF GRATITUDE

■

Prayer is not the only time-tested kindling for the fire of godly enthusiasm. There is also the attitude of gratitude, and it builds upon both a healthy image of God and a vibrant, intentional prayer life.

As David Steindl-Rast, OSB, so wisely states on his popular web site, www.gratefulness.org, "In daily life we must see that it is not happiness that makes us grateful, but gratefulness that makes us happy." Gratitude transforms us into children who recognize their dependence and who realize that everything is a grace, gift, and blessing from a good God. In God's generous bidding to have a relationship with us, God spreads before us an exquisite table called the banquet of life and offers us everything we need. God enthusiastically invites, "Come to the feast!" As invited guests to this banquet, we can never point to anything and say, "This is mine"—except for our sins. Everything else comes from the generosity of God.

G. K. Chesterton, the English writer and Christian apologist, wrote, "You say grace before meals. All right. But I say grace before the concert and the opera, and grace before the play and pantomime, and grace before I open a book, and grace before sketching, painting, swimming, fencing, boxing, walking, playing, dancing and grace before I dip the pen in the ink."[7] God's grace is the unquestionable foundation of life, and gratitude is the first response.

That realization gave a unique twist to the poverty of Francis of Assisi. Unlike the monastic understanding of his time, which interpreted poverty as a form of self-denial, Francis's poverty was born of a radical affirmation that God can be trusted to provide for everything—from a helping hand in times of loneliness to food, clothing, and shelter.

Toward the end of his life, Francis reflected upon his forty-four years and wrote unabashedly in his *Testament* how God was always ready to provide for his needs. No less than four times he uses the expression, "The Lord gave me. . . ." All was gift and grace: the beginning of his conversion and ministry to the lepers, his faith, his respect for priests, and the brothers who joined him. Awareness of God's providence not only fueled Francis's understanding of poverty and his attitude of gratitude, but it is also a stunning reminder to us that worry and anxiety are insults to God.

Obstacles to a Grateful Heart

The crippling effects of worry and anxiety are not the only obstacles to gratitude. I note two others. The first is that many of us are so busy multitasking that we never stop long enough to reflect and become aware of the many people, events, and situations the Spirit uses to touch us and transform our lives. I tend to do this myself.

At least twice a month, I pack a bag, get into a taxi, and head to the airport to catch a flight. That forty-minute ride would provide an excellent time to sit back and reflect upon my life. But instead of thinking and praying about how God is speaking to me in these airport trips and my ministry, I usually spend the time checking my e-mails, updating my radio show's Facebook page, revising my presentations, and replying to voicemail messages. Socrates might have been speaking directly to me when he said, "The unexamined life is not worth living"! My multitasking reveals a root cause of ingratitude.

The second additional obstacle to gratitude comes when we too often forget how God's grace and goodness helped us through past tragedies and major disappointments. We fail to recognize and remember how God cares for us in our small, daily routines. To ignore or forget God's goodness to us, or to give credit to anyone else, is to begin writing a work of historical fiction.

Growing in Gratitude

Since I have struggled in the past to give gratitude the attention it deserves, let me tell you what I have learned. There are practices that are helpful in fostering a spirit of gratefulness and appreciation, that make our lives worry-free and happier.

The French say that "gratitude is the memory of the heart." And memory is forged with *daily reflection and mindful awareness*. One of my spiritual directees spends ten minutes a day reflecting upon her life and remembering the many ways God has blessed her. Sometimes she surveys the broad strokes of her fifty years of life; other times she sits in gratitude and praise for a surprise visit from a friend, a sunny day, or a freshly brewed cup of coffee. She continually tells me that daily reflection and mindful awareness help to expand her heart as she comes to see the utter gratuity of the marvelous and the mundane.

The Jewish theologian Abraham Joshua Heschel once walked into his New York classroom and announced, "An incredible thing happened as I was walking over here to class." This comment piqued the curiosity of his students, who asked what he'd seen. Heschel responded, "The sun set. The sun set and no one on Broadway noticed it."[8]

Heschel reminds us of the importance of *wonder and awe*. When we take the time to reflect not just on our life's journey but on life itself, we get a sense of the magic in the air. And that drives us to our knees in thanks. The fingernails of a newborn baby, a shooting star streaking across the sky, the oddity of a Venus fly trap, the howling of a coyote, and the beauty of the Alps pull us out of ourselves and reveal something bigger than ourselves. And that "something" is a Creator who is enthusiastic about being in a relationship with us.

When I look at your heavens, the work of your fingers, the moon and the stars that you have established; what are human beings that you are mindful of them, mortals that you care for them?

(Psalm 8:3–4)

The magnificent creativity of God and our awe at the lavishness of life lead us to an awareness of who we really are. Knowing that we are invited guests to the banquet of life fuels the virtue of *humility* that grounds all gratitude. Derived from the Latin word *humus*, meaning dirt or ground, humility keeps our feet on the ground as it raises up our eyes to God in thanks and praise. There is no authentic gratitude without the awareness of our unworthiness and insignificance.

Living in a world of progress reports, report cards, and performance evaluations, we are often tempted to take ourselves too seriously. What would it feel like to rediscover a childlike sense of *joy and playfulness* that connects you to the inherent goodness of life? A game of pitch-and-catch with an eight-year-old son? Playing house with a niece? Making up a bedtime story, walking the dog, finding a coworker to play Rock-Paper-Scissors, going for a swim, or dressing up with hat and boots and square dancing with a spouse? These activities can be spiritual practices that open us to a dimension of life that we, as adults, don't often experience. Far from a cynical question, "Are we having fun yet?" is an excellent reminder of the importance of joy and laughter. The great Teresa of Avila rightly reminded her community that a sad nun is a bad nun. We grow old and ungrateful when we stop playing, teasing, and laughing.

Gratitude and appreciation form the warp and weft of every invited guest's clothing. They are so basic and essential for our transformation into little Christs that Meister Eckhart, a fourteenth-century Dominican mystic, said, "If the only prayer you ever say in your entire life is thank you, it will be enough."

■ REFLECT

1. How has a spirit of gratitude shaped your lifestyle and spiritual practice? When are you more prone to gratitude? To ingratitude?
2. Where does pride still reign in your life? Why?
3. When and how was the last time you played and laughed? Did it help foster a spirit of gratitude and appreciation for life? How can playfulness and joy be better incorporated into your spiritual journey?

■ GO DEEPER

Angeles Arrien, *Living in Gratitude: A Journey That Will Change Your Life* (Boulder, CO: Sounds True, 2011).

Wilkie Au and Noreen Cannon Au, *The Grateful Heart: Living the Christian Message* (Mahwah, NJ: Paulist Press, 2011).

Albert Haase, OFM, "The Importance of Gratitude," http://www
.youtube.com/watch?v=PcPyv_Y0h_g.

David Steindl-Rast, *Gratefulness, The Heart of Prayer: An Approach
to Life in Fullness* (Mahwah, NJ: Paulist Press, 1984).

CHAPTER 9

THE DIVINE MILIEU

∎

Yesterday, while giving spiritual direction and reflecting upon this chapter's topic, I asked several people where they find God. I was surprised to get many different answers. Belinda said, "I see God in the second-grade children I teach. Their innocence, joy, and wonder often remind me that God is closer than I have ever thought or imagined." Mike, a Protestant minister, replied, "I find God in Scripture. In his Word, God reveals to me his divine love and forgiveness. In my opinion, that's all we need in life." Sister Catherine, a pastoral associate in a large suburban Catholic parish, said, "I find God within. Years ago I read a mystic who talked about the 'sanctuary of the soul,' and so every day I spend time in prayer, going within to encounter my God." Bill, who is legally blind, replied, "I see God in the gift of the Eucharist."

The Divine Milieu

As I listened to these replies, I couldn't help remembering Augustine's definition of a sacrament: "a visible sign of an invisible reality."[9] My directees' different answers and Augustine's definition make me aware that, in a broad sense, our existence is sacramental: many earthly realities reveal God's existence, God's merciful compassion, and God's urgent longing to be in a relationship with us. We live in a "divine milieu," to borrow a phrase from the Jesuit philosopher and paleontologist Pierre Teilhard de Chardin.

He is the image of the invisible God, the firstborn of all creation. . . . For in him all the fullness of God was pleased to dwell.

(Colossians 1:15, 19)

Two thousand years ago, God walked this earth in the person of Jesus called Emmanuel, "God is with us" (Matthew 1:23), love made flesh. "Whoever has seen me has seen the Father" (John 14:9). Jesus is not only the full manifestation of God on the spiritual journey but also is himself the path. "I am the way. . . . No one comes to the Father except through me" (John 14:6).

We are not at a disadvantage in meeting Jesus simply because we live in the twenty-first century. We too can encounter him in another way that boggles my mind and that I don't always appreciate: in the poor, the marginalized, and those who have no voice in society. "Truly I tell you, just as you did it to one of the least of these who are members of my family, you did it to me" (Matthew 25:40); "Whoever welcomes this child in my name welcomes me, and whoever welcomes me welcomes the one who sent me" (Luke 9:48). Those who have no personal resources to fall back upon and who live with outstretched hands reveal the humility of God who was born in a stable and died on a cross.

The gathered Christian community—the church—also continues the presence of Jesus in our midst: "For where two or three are gathered in my name, I am there among them" (Matthew 18:20). The love shown to our neighbors and that we are blessed to receive from others, the forgiveness both offered and obtained, and the merciful compassion that wells up in the hearts of believers, all are fragmentary expressions of God's unfathomable love, forgiveness, and compassion revealed in Jesus.

Furthermore, as embodied spirits with the gifts of self-awareness, reflection, and creativity, we mirror in our limited, human way the image of God (Genesis 1:27). We are also temples of God's indwelling Spirit (1 Corinthians 3:16), who seeks to transform us ever more into little Christs. In a word, we ourselves are visible signs of an invisible reality.

Sacraments and Scripture

We also encounter the continuing ministry of Christ in the sacraments of the Church. There, Jesus is fully alive! The *Catechism of the Catholic Church* defines sacraments as "efficacious signs of grace, instituted by Christ and entrusted to the Church, by which divine life is dispensed to us" (#1131). These actions of the Church make present ("efficacious signs") an encounter with God ("grace"). They are heavenly treasures on earth. Each of them is rooted in the life and ministry of Jesus: his baptism in the Jordan (baptism); his forgiveness of sins (reconciliation); his gift of the Holy Spirit to aid us in our mission (confirmation); his healing ministry (anointing of the sick); his first miracle at Cana recorded in the Gospel of John (matrimony); his choice of Peter and the apostles (sacerdotal and episcopal ordination); his table ministry and last supper before his death (Eucharist). Though Christian denominations disagree on the exact number of the sacraments instituted by Christ, they do agree that using ordinary things such as water, oil, a gesture, bread and wine, under certain conditions, provides sparks for the fire of godly enthusiasm in our lives.

And then we encounter the divine in the Scriptures. In the written word of God, the Father of creation tells us about his burning desire to be in a relationship with us; that is what salvation history is all about. In the pages of Scripture we come face-to-face with our vocation to become little Christs sent to respond lovingly to the needs or duties set before us. Unlike contemporary novels and short stories, Scripture is "living and active, sharper than any two-edged sword" (Hebrews 4:12), used by the Spirit as a tool in the process of our transformation.

The Books of Creation and Life

If sacraments are visible signs of invisible realities, then creation too is sacramental; its qualities and design betray the creativity and wisdom of its author. Some have even referred to it as a book written by God. Though there is a clear distinction between the Creator and creation, all created things, such as trees, wild rabbits, and turnips, bear the signature of the Creator and give us a glimmer of God; indeed, every page of this book has been handwritten by the divine. No wonder the Franciscan mystic Angela of Foligno said that the world was "pregnant with God."[10]

Celtic spirituality offers beautiful reflections and interpretations of how this works. These ancient Christian teachings propose that some places are especially *thin*, meaning that here the supposed wall separating the divine from the human is exceptionally low and permeable. Perhaps you have felt this at some time in your own life. I experienced this in an extraordinary way when I walked the grounds of Dachau concentration camp and felt the grief of God. I again felt God's majesty as I flew over the vast Sahara desert, and then later God's abiding presence while praying in Chartres cathedral. I've also experienced the divine presence in the silence of a local forest preserve and at the graves of my parents in New Orleans. Whether natural landscapes or holy places of pilgrimage made by human hands, these locations and others are the meeting grounds for God and the human race; in these places we palpably experience the closeness of the divine.

All of these—the person of Jesus, a neighbor in need or in the church, our physical bodies, the Church's sacraments, Scripture, creation, and thin places—provide glimmers of God, reminding us that we live in a divine milieu. This awareness is further kindling that has the potential to set us ablaze.

■ REFLECT

1. Where do you typically "find" God? How do you respond to the divine presence in your life?

2. Of the visible realities pointing to God mentioned in this chapter—Jesus, a neighbor in need or in the church, our physical bodies, the sacraments, Scripture, creation, and thin places—which one do you find the most challenging? The most comforting?

3. When was the last time you felt the closeness of God? Where were you? What feelings did it elicit from you?

■ GO DEEPER

Mindie Burgoyne, "Walking through Thin Places," http://www
.thinplaces.net/openingarticle.htm.

Pierre Teilhard de Chardin, *The Divine Milieu (Perennial Classics)*
(New York: Harper, 2001).

Mary Margaret Funk, OSB, *Lectio Matters before the Burning Bush:
Through the Revelatory Texts of Scripture, Nature and Experience*
(New York: Continuum, 2010).

Joseph J. Martos, *Doors to the Sacred: A Historical Introduction to
Sacraments in the Catholic Church*, Revised and Updated (Chicago:
Triumph Books, 2001).

CHAPTER 10

ME, MYSELF, AND I: True or False?

■

During a spiritual direction session, a directee once said to me, "I so easily identify with Saint Paul when he says, 'I do not understand my own actions. For I do not do what I want, but I do the very thing I hate'" (Romans 7:15).

When I asked her to explain, she said, "I love to buy handbags. And I know it! I also know that I have too many handbags for anyone to use. So I really try and stop myself from buying more of them. But then, all of a sudden, if I am a little bit sad or if I need a little emotional lift—after all, we're supposed to be happy, right?—I see this stranger get into her car, drive to the mall, and buy another handbag. And that stranger, believe it or not, is *me*! I just don't understand. I know the thrill of buying another handbag isn't going to last forever, but I keep thinking it will, and so I keep doing it."

I thought it most interesting and right on target that she referred to "this stranger." In her own way, she was experiencing what we call the "false self."

The Energy Centers of the False Self

There is a demanding, irrational, and sometimes spoiled stranger inside each one of us. And this stranger often tries to throw water on our kindling by convincing us to do things we know better not to do or often don't want to do.

Taking an expression made popular by Thomas Merton in his writings from the 1960s, another Trappist monk, Thomas Keating, ocso, calls this stranger inside us the "false self." This false self is obsessed with self-concern, self-interest, self-gratification, and self-preservation. It equates happiness with satisfying the instinctual needs of these self-obsessions by running after power and control, survival and security, a need for affection, the desire for esteem and pleasure, and cultural or group identification. Keating sometimes refers to these needs as the "emotional energy centers."

Some adults become obsessed with power and control, seeking endless ways to amass prestige, dominate others, and impose their wills. Some are never satisfied with their bank accounts or possessions, greedily chasing after big money, gadgets, and stuff. Still others go on a quixotic search for love and self-esteem, looking in all the wrong places, whether it be dimly lit street corners or the approving smiles of anyone or everyone. And still others find strength in numbers, joining organizations and groups of people with varying agendas—just as long as it gives a sense of approval, acceptance, and most of all, inclusion.

These energy centers get solidified early in life, and somewhere along the line, as we live without self-reflection, we become convinced that we *need* to satisfy one or more of them *in order to be happy*. Yes, we all need some power, security, and love to have healthy adult self-images. But the false self takes that to the extreme and persuades us of its deceptive agenda: happiness comes *solely* from the emotional lift provided by buying a handbag, joining groups or being with other people, or feeling love. As soon as that emotional energy center has been momentarily satisfied, the thrill dissipates, and we see that we have once again been double-crossed and conned. This struggle with the deception of the false self is lifelong for anyone preparing kindling for the spark from God.

I've discovered that the false self isn't just invested in acquiring "empty P's" like power, possessions, pleasure, and popularity. It's also insistent on avoiding pain, blame, criticism, disgrace, and loss. Criticize me or try and inflict emotional pain on me—and you'll instantly hear me justifying, denying, rationalizing, shaming, and finger pointing. In many respects, the false self is the ventriloquist of the inner monologue and, when threatened, will not hesitate to move its lips to verbally defend itself.

The obsession to satisfy the desires of the energy centers and to avoid any kind of pain and criticism keeps the false self alive. That stranger continues to influence and dominate our lives as long as we indulge its agenda.

Jesus and the True Self

Jesus directly confronted the false self's agenda to acquire comforts and avoid pain. On a number of occasions, he taught a new way of living, freed from the stranglehold of the false self:

> Do not resist the evil-doer. But if anyone strikes you on the right cheek, turn the other also; and if anyone wants to sue you and take your coat, give your cloak as well; and if anyone forces you to go one mile, go also the second mile.
>
> (Matthew 5:39–41)

- "Do not fear those who kill the body but cannot kill the soul; rather fear him who can destroy both soul and body in hell" (Matthew 10:28).
- "Therefore I tell you, do not worry about your life, what you will eat or what you will drink, or about your

body, what you will wear. Is not life more than food, and the body more than clothing?" (Matthew 6:25).

- "If any want to become my followers, let them deny themselves and take up their cross daily and follow me" (Luke 9:23).
- "Love your enemies and pray for those who persecute you" (Matthew 5:44).

The Spirit acts upon this wisdom of Jesus as the Spirit disengages us from the self-serving agenda of the false self and transforms us into little Christs sent to live with radical trust in God and uncompromising love of neighbor. This is the "true self," the person God intends for us to be, and is characterized by the fruit of the Spirit: "love, joy, peace, patience, kindness, generosity, faithfulness, gentleness, and self-control" (Galatians 5:22–23).

Yet the false self protests against this transformation, pushes back, and resists. And that resistance is based upon fear. The false self is terrified of a life without the emotional highs of power, prestige, possessions, and popularity; it dreads a life of pain and disgrace.

That resistance gets translated into emotional frustration as we struggle to satisfy the energy centers and defend ourselves against any kind of criticism or loss. Ever wonder why you feel so frustrated? Much of it is self-imposed as you doggedly cling to the false self's egocentric agenda and refuse the transformation offered by the Spirit.

The Beatitudes of Jesus as presented in Matthew (5:3–11) offer us a way to break free of the self-imposed frustration caused by our preoccupation and to prepare kindling for the spark of the Spirit:

- Attacking the selfish agenda of the false self head-on, Jesus tells those of us who are obsessed with possessions and pride,

"Blessed are the poor in spirit, for theirs is the kingdom of heaven" (verse 3).

- Those of us on the hunt for emotional highs and pleasure are reminded, "Blessed are those who mourn, for they will be comforted" (verse 4).
- An obsession with power will not give us what we think it will: "Blessed are the meek, for they will inherit the earth" (verse 5).
- We miss the mark when we try and dodge the criticism and disgrace that comes with standing up for the truth: "Blessed are those who hunger and thirst for righteousness, for they will be filled" (verse 6).
- A duplicitous life of serving the agenda of the false self while trying to become a little Christ clouds one's vision: "Blessed are the pure in heart, for they will see God" (verse 8).
- Those who are aggressive, defensive, and seek revenge are warned, "Blessed are the merciful, for they will receive mercy," and "Blessed are the peacemakers, for they will be called children of God" (verses 7, 9).
- And there is an ultimate and lasting payoff for those who submit to pain, blame, criticism, and disgrace: "Blessed are you when people revile you and persecute you and utter all kinds of evil against you falsely on my account. Rejoice and be glad, for your reward is great in heaven, for in the same way they persecuted the prophets who were before you" (verses 11–12).

With a succinct pointedness, the Beatitudes clearly demonstrate that there is a new kind of logic at work as the Spirit begins the process of transforming us into little Christs. By living the Beatitudes and using Jesus's wisdom as kindling, we facilitate the Spirit's action of setting our lives on fire.

▪ REFLECT

1. What do you think you *need* in order to be happy? How is this belief a source of anxiety and frustration in your life?

2. What methods and techniques do you use to avoid pain, blame, criticism, disgrace, and loss? Why do you refuse to accept these things?

3. How do the Beatitudes of Jesus challenge your current thoughts and actions? Which of them speaks the most to you?

▪ GO DEEPER

Albert Haase, OFM, *Coming Home to Your True Self: Leaving the Emptiness of False Attractions* (Downers Grove, IL: InterVarsity Press, 2008).

Albert Haase, OFM, "The Challenge of the Ego," http://www.youtube .com/watch?v=yBrN9QDpROM.

Thomas Keating, *Foundations for Centering Prayer and the Christian Contemplative Life; Open Mind, Open Heart; Invitation to Love; The Mystery of Christ* (New York: Continuum, 2002).

CHAPTER 11

GOD AND SUFFERING

▪

Widowed at the age of forty-seven by my father's suicide, my mother had only a high school diploma, no professional skills, a debt of $60,000, and three of her five children left at home still to raise. By God's grace coupled with her sacrificial spirit and innate tenacity, she would attend the college graduation of her three boys and retire as a computer administrator for an insurance company. All five of her children had hoped her retirement would be filled with the joys of being a grandmother and the pride of having two daughters in the convent and one son an ordained priest.

But her retirement didn't turn out that way. It was marred by confusion and erratic mood swings. Alzheimer's disease began to blanket this once feisty, vivacious woman and reduce her to smoldering ashes.

As I watched her life flame out, I often asked, why did God allow someone who had suffered so much to come to such an undignified end? Why did God allow my mother to suffer for so many years with the gnawing guilt of a spouse's suicide? Why hadn't God intervened and performed a miracle to ease her emotional suffering and physical hardships?

My mother had chosen to be cremated. When the funeral director handed me the small square urn that contained her ashes, I wondered, why doesn't God improve his reputation and respond to requests to alleviate suffering in the world? It would certainly entice and excite others to follow the Spirit more intentionally.

Scripture and Suffering

We all have had the experience of praying to God and asking why. Why do children suffer? Why doesn't God stop wars? Why doesn't God intervene and stop us from enduring pain, misery, misfortune, and affliction?

These questions, left unanswered by God, have been asked since the beginning of time and often are used by some people to justify a cold disinterest in personal spiritual transformation. Further, the different and diverse answers that some people have given don't always sit well with us even though they can be justified with reference to the Scriptures. Some of the typical scriptural answers include:

- *God uses suffering as punishment for sin.* The Old Testament begins with God punishing the original parents' disobedience with the pangs of childbirth and the toil of labor (see Genesis 3:16–19). The books of Judges, Samuel, Kings, and many of the prophets amplify this idea by portraying God as a judge who blesses the chosen people with prosperity and success when they are faithful but quickly punishes when they turn away and begin to worship idols. According to this interpretation, God's severest punishment came with the chosen people's exile from the promised land: "And the nations shall know that the house of Israel went into captivity for their iniquity, because they dealt treacherously with me [says the LORD God]" (Ezekiel 39:23).

- *God is not the cause.* Jesus distances his Abba from the image of a judge who punishes those who sin. His father shows no favoritism, since he lets the sun rise on the good and the evil and sends rain on the righteous and the unrighteous (see Matthew 5:45). He dismisses the idea that suffering or sickness is a punishment for sin (see Luke 13:1–5; John 9:3). However, he makes clear that discipleship does not insulate us from potential pain and suffering; it involves taking up our crosses and losing our lives for his and the gospel's sake (see Mark 8:34–35).

- *Suffering is good even though we cannot always see why.* Scripture sometimes highlights how God brings good out of suffering. In the Old Testament, Joseph saw how God had used his suffering for the greater good of numerous people (see Genesis 50:15–21). In the New Testament, Peter, echoing Isaiah's suffering servant (see Isaiah 53:4–5), interprets Christ's suffering as the very means of our redemption: "[Christ] himself bore our sins in his body on the cross, so that, free from sins, we might live for righteousness; by his wounds you have been healed" (1 Peter 2:24).

- *Suffering can be a form of God's discipline.* Proverbs states that suffering is the discipline and reproof of a loving God (see Proverbs 3:11–12). The letter to the Hebrews comments explicitly on this proverb and highlights the transformative powers of this kind of discipline: the Father of spirits "disciplines us for our good, in order that we may share his holiness" (Hebrews 12:10).

- *Suffering can be character building.* Though he does not mention God's role in it, Paul notes the pride we should take in suffering, since it builds up in us endurance, character, and hope (Romans 5:1–5).

- *The devil causes suffering.* The New Testament offers still another interpretation of suffering. God's enemy, the demons (Luke 9:38–39), evil spirits (Acts 19:11–12), Satan (Luke 13:16) or the devil (Acts 10:38), are sometimes depicted in ways that make it seem that they are the cause of all sickness and diseases.

Our Response

You can clearly see that there isn't one consistent scriptural answer for the question, why suffering? Each of these answers occasionally can be helpful, while in some circumstances—like African starvation, AIDS, Alzheimer's disease, or the death of a loved one—they might seem blatantly cruel. A few might be helpful for you but not for me. Some might make sense only in hindsight; others might seem totally senseless or downright silly.

Trying to come to terms with an adequate answer to the question of suffering is doomed to frustration and maybe even failure. The book of Job attempts to answer it and, frankly, comes up short. I've racked my brains for years and have read virtually every book on the topic and I still walk around with this question gnawing in my heart.

I'm often accused of opting out of any discussion on the reason for suffering. Rather than trying to answer the question *why*, which might only satisfy the intellectually curious, perhaps the more important questions to ask are: *How* do we live with the mystery of suffering? *How* do we prepare kindling for the spark from a supposedly loving God when agony or distress has blanketed our soul? Here, the biblical tradition does, in fact, offer us some helpful answers.

Face the suffering and cry out. We typically shy away from suffering. We do our best to medicate ourselves against it, often encouraging each other to keep a stiff upper lip and, "Don't worry, be happy."

My God, my God, why
have you forsaken me?
Why are you so far from
helping me, from the
words of my groaning?
O my God, I cry by day,
but you do not answer;
and by night, but find no
rest. . . .
In you our ancestors
trusted; they trusted,
and you delivered them.
To you they cried, and
were saved; in you they
trusted, and were not
put to shame.

(Psalm 22:1–2,
4–5)

Scripture, however, challenges us to face the suffering and lament. Psalms such as 3, 5, 10, 17, 22, 38, 44, 77, 88, and 109 suggest we cry out to God from the depths of our sadness and pain. Far from betraying disbelief or doubt in God, the prayer of lament is actually a profound expression of trust in God's ultimate power and vindication. That's why we shouldn't fear divine anger or retribution when praying it.

Hang on to faith in God. Lamenting allows us to stay connected to God with even the thinnest thread of faith. Psalm 22 reminds us that faith is sometimes mined in hindsight, by remembering times past when our or others' prayers were answered: "To you [our ancestors] cried, and were saved" (verse 5).

The encouragement of Scripture is that God gives heed to hope fashioned out of helplessness (Psalm 138:3; 2 Corinthians 1:8–11; Philippians 1:19–20). Anguish raised in prayer is always addressed by Providence.

Surrender. As we lament in our anguish, we must also realize that suffering is often a mystery. Though

Christian responsibility and prudence challenge us to extricate ourselves from abusive situations or follow the wise advice of medical science, some forms of suffering we can only bow before—and willingly submit to. Standing before the ineffable God who controls the seeming chaos of creation (see Job 38–40), with Job we say, "I'm speechless, in awe—words fail me. I should never have opened my mouth!" (40:4, THE MESSAGE). With Shadrach, Meshach, and Abednego, we walk through the fiery furnace trusting that it is a furnace of transformation as we pray their prayer: "And now with all our heart we follow you; we fear you and seek your presence. Do not put us to shame, but deal with us in your patience and in your abundant mercy. Deliver us in accordance with your marvelous works, and bring glory to your name, O Lord" (Daniel 3:41–43). Surrendering to suffering, indeed, is the ultimate act of faith and trust for a little Christ: "Father, into your hands I commend my spirit" (Luke 23:46).

Far from a problem to be solved or understood, suffering will inevitably shape and mold the contours of our souls. Facing, lamenting, and surrendering to it with even the thinnest threads of faith and trust becomes an inspired moment that provides kindling for godly enthusiasm during the most difficult of times.

■ REFLECT

1. How can a God of unconditional love permit suffering? How satisfying is your answer?

2. Which of the scriptural understandings of suffering ring true to your own experience? Which ones do not?

3. Reflect upon a recent moment of suffering. How did you initially respond? Have you learned anything about suffering in hindsight?

■ GO DEEPER

Randy Alcorn, *If God Is Good: Faith in the Midst of Suffering and Evil* (Colorado Springs, CO: Multnomah Books, 2009).

Albert Haase, OFM, "Keeping Faith in Difficult Times," http://www.youtube.com/watch?v=Fg5Xk2ejlOQ.

Kenneth R. Overberg, SJ, "The Mystery of Suffering: How Should I Respond?" http://www.americancatholic.org/newsletters/cu/ac0702.asp.

Jerry Sittser, *A Grace Disguised: How the Soul Grows through Loss* (Grand Rapids, MI: Zondervan, 2004).

CATCHING
FIRE

METHODS OF PRAYER

■

God's fiery passion sparks kindling into flame
through a rich variety of prayer methods that
stoke the awareness of God's presence in our
ordinary lives.

CHAPTER 12

THE EXAMEN

■

One day a discouraged Christian who hadn't given much attention to his relationship with God asked the fourteenth-century Dominican mystic Meister Eckhart for a suggestion about how to make up for lost time. Eckhart replied, "Be in all things a God-seeker and at all times, a God-finder, among all kinds of people and in all kinds of circumstances. And make it a life habit to copy Jesus Christ, to do the things he did and avoid the things he avoided."[11]

You might be noticing some smoldering embers inside of you. They might be glowing with the desire for transformation so you can seek and find God in all the people and circumstances you encounter. You might be wondering how to kindle those embers into flame.

Or maybe you feel like that discouraged Christian who hadn't given much attention to spiritual growth. You want to cut to the chase by finding out about spiritual practices and how to catch fire.

In either case, let's start talking about deepening our response to God.

There is a vast array of spiritual practices from which to choose. Our personality plays a big role in determining which practice or technique warms us spiritually. No one is capable of simultaneously practicing all the techniques that I'll be discussing or even finding them all helpful—and, thankfully, we are not supposed to. So pick and choose. By trial and error, you'll gradually discover which ones help you yield to the Spirit's transformation.

There is no better place to start than the Examen. Being God-seekers and God-finders is the basis of this five-hundred-year-old prayer method. People nowadays refer to the Examen as the examination of consciousness. It consists of reviewing and surveying our ordinary routine and the mundane messiness of our daily lives; this intentional practice often reveals divine sparks in the people, events, meetings, and circumstances we have just experienced. That awareness can set us on fire with godly enthusiasm.

The Practice

Saint Ignatius of Loyola is credited with proposing and promoting the Examen. He taught that it should be done twice daily, at midday and again before retiring to bed. However, his flexibility also allows for a once-daily practice. For some, mornings work better than evenings. Ignatius also taught that it should not extend excessively; fifteen to twenty minutes is ample time to reap its benefits if it is done faithfully and daily.

There are five steps to the traditional practice of the Examen. Again, Ignatius allows for flexibility. After some practice, we can adapt and tweak the steps, realizing that the goal is to become increasingly aware and conscious of the divine presence in our everyday lives. Perhaps, on some days, a person would focus on just one or two of the steps; on other days, she would complete all five steps within the allotted time frame. The benefits of the practice are reaped in daily fidelity to it, not simply in getting through each of the five individual steps.

The first step of the Examen is *gratitude*. We look over our present life and thank God for any gifts, graces, or blessings we have received. This step of gratitude might focus on life's big picture and the many manifestations of God's love: spouse, children, job, home, or the inner strength that seemingly came out of nowhere to help us get through a crisis or an emotional upheaval. At other times, our gratitude might be focused like a laser beam on a specific person, event, or grace that was given to us as recently as a few hours ago. We should not be too quick to move on from this step, since growth in gratitude is growth in the conscious awareness of God's generosity to us.

My twenty-minute practice of the Examen consists solely of this first step at times. Gratitude and thanksgiving sometimes race across my soul like wildfire as I become conscious of God's encouragement and support spoken through the words of a friend or relative. Or I become attuned in a conscious way to God's gift of a sunny day, a phone call from a close friend, or an insight that God allowed me to put into words. The flames of gratitude leap up and I bask in their warmth—and in their long afterglow.

Step two is the *petition to the Holy Spirit*. Since the Spirit is the flint and fuel of godly enthusiasm and the One who transforms us into little Christs, we ask the Holy Spirit to open up our eyes, ears, and hearts as we review the events of the past few hours since our last practice of the Examen. This is also a prayer for enlightenment and insight as we seek to understand the many and varied ways the Spirit of God calls us to spiritual transformation. This petition helps to bring the Holy Spirit front and center to our consciousness.

The Heart of the Examen

While they were talking and discussing, Jesus himself came near and went with them, but their eyes were kept from recognizing him. . . . Then their eyes were opened, and they recognized him; and he vanished from their sight.

(Luke 24:15–16, 31)

The *review* forms the heart and soul of the Examen. We survey and probe the immediate past hours since the last time we practiced the Examen. Event by event, hour by hour, minute by minute, we pray through the day "rummaging for God,"[12] as one writer describes it. Questions that we ask ourselves include:

- Where was God speaking to me and challenging me?
- How was the Spirit inviting me to be more Christlike?
- When and in what circumstances was God bestowing graces, gifts, and blessings upon me?
- How was the Spirit asking me to be lovingly present in the situation in which I found myself?
- How was God asking me to humbly serve the people in front of me?

It's important to remember that this third step is God-centered, not me-centered. That's why the Examen is called an examination of consciousness and is distinct from an examination of conscience: we look for God in the Examen and do not judge ourselves, as in an examination of conscience.

The fourth step is asking for *forgiveness*. We express sorrow and ask forgiveness for still living on autopilot, unaware and unconscious of God's surrounding presence in the daily routines. This step is not supposed to be a monologue in which we scold and criticize ourselves for our insensitivity or put ourselves on a guilt trip. Rather, this step is intended to be a dialogue between God and ourselves in which we encounter a merciful, loving God who is enthusiastic about being in a relationship with us. If we walk away from this step feeling guilty or remorseful, we might not have allowed enough time to hear the consoling and forgiving words of God.

The Examen concludes with the *renewal*. In this step, we look over our upcoming daily schedule as we now know it and anticipate the approaching hours or events where we need to be particularly attentive to the pending manifestation of the divine presence or call. We anticipate God's presence in order to participate in it. We ask ourselves:

- Where might the God of disguise surprise me?
- What situation might the Spirit use to mold me ever closer into a little Christ?
- How could God possibly use this particular person or this planned meeting to spark my godly enthusiasm into flame?

In this fifth and final step, we are recommitting ourselves to switching our lives off autopilot.

For over six years, I have practiced the Examen daily. I find this simple method of prayer extraordinarily helpful in transforming me into a God-seeker, a God-finder, and someone who is aware that "[God] is not far from each one of us. For 'In him we live and move and have our being'" (Acts 17:27–28). Thanks to the Examen, I am convinced that God's passion to have a relationship with me spills over into the mundane moments of my everyday routine.

■ REFLECT

1. How often in the past week do you think you were living on autopilot? What practical ways can you adopt to become a more conscious God-seeker and God-finder?

2. Spend some time right now rummaging for God over the past few hours. How difficult do you find this to be? How do you know it's really God and not just your imagination?

3. Which of the five specific steps of the Examen would help you catch the flame of godly enthusiasm most of all? Is there anything stopping you from practicing the Examen, and that step, now?

■ GO DEEPER

Timothy M. Gallagher, OMV, *The Examen Prayer: Ignatian Wisdom for Our Lives Today* (New York: Crossroad, 2006).

Jim Manney, *A Simple Life-Changing Prayer: Discovering the Power of St. Ignatius Loyola's Examen* (Chicago: Loyola Press, 2011).

CHAPTER 13

MEDITATION AND CONTEMPLATION

■

Peter had been coming to spiritual direction for about six months. During one session he admitted, "I think I am losing ground in the spiritual life and going backward. For a few months, I had felt that God was really listening to my prayer, and I was making progress. But recently I find myself not having too much to say. And as strange as it sounds, I don't *want* to say anything. I just want to sit there and do nothing. What am I doing wrong?"

It quickly became apparent to me that God was inviting Peter into a more meditative or contemplative style of prayer.

"The Pure, Loving Gaze"

It's a common phenomenon: the more we pray, the less we say. And the less we say, the more the Spirit has the opportunity to shape and transform our prayer (see Romans 8:26). Our relationship with God is like any other relationship: the more time we spend with God in prayer, the less need we have to talk and the more we simply desire to be silent and attentive to the presence of the divine. "Be still, and know that I am God" (Psalm 46:10) is the Spirit's advice as we catch the fire of godly enthusiasm and develop a history of prayer time with God.

This stillness, silence, and attentiveness can lead to "the pure, loving gaze that finds God everywhere,"[13] to use the words of the seventeenth-century Carmelite Brother Lawrence of the Resurrection. Like any lover, we just lovingly bask in the presence of the beloved with no words or thoughts. This loving gaze is really the heart of meditative and contemplative prayer.

There are two popular methods of meditation and contemplation, slightly different from each other, that help facilitate the pure, loving gaze of God and are quite helpful at a certain stage in the spiritual journey. One is promoted by the late John Main, OSB, Laurence Freeman, OSB, and the World Community of Christian Meditation (www.wccm-usa.org). The other is promoted by Thomas Keating, OCSO, and the Contemplative Outreach (www.contemplativeoutreach .org).

Each method suggests the use of a sacred word or mantra as a way of distancing ourselves from distractions and focusing our attention. The word or mantra should have no visual connotation or elicit from us any emotional response, since any associated meaning or feeling would distract us from our still, silent, and attentive gaze upon God.

The method taught and promoted by the World Community of Christian Meditation is as follows:

1. Sit down. Sit still and upright. Close your eyes lightly. Sit relaxed but alert. Breathe calmly and regularly.

2. Silently, interiorly begin to say a single word. They recommend the prayer-phrase MA-RA-NA-THA (the Aramaic expression, probably used in the early Christian liturgy, meaning "Our Lord, come!" or "Our Lord has come!" See 1 Corinthians 16:22 and Revelation 22:20). Recite it as four syllables of equal length. Listen to it as you say it, gently but continuously.

3. Do not think or imagine anything—spiritual or otherwise.

4. If thoughts and images come, these are distractions at the time of meditation, so keep returning to the simple repetition of the word.

5. Meditate each morning and evening for twenty to thirty minutes.

The method taught and promoted by Contemplative Outreach is as follows:

1. Choose a sacred word as the symbol of your intention to consent to God's presence and action within. I myself find the word "Presence" to be most helpful. Some people use "Father," "Abba," "Jesus," "Mercy," among others.

2. Sitting comfortably and with eyes closed, settle briefly, and silently introduce the sacred word as the symbol of your consent to God's presence and action within.

3. When engaged with or distracted by your thoughts (which include body sensations, feelings, images, and reflections), return ever so gently to the sacred word.

4. At the end of the prayer period, remain in silence with eyes closed for a couple of minutes.

Note that in these methods the sacred word is used in two different ways. In meditation, the word is used with slow and gentle repetition. Like the repetition of the "Hail Mary" when praying the rosary or the slow methodical beating of a drum, its role is to help us stay alert as we focus our attention and energies on the divine presence. In the second method promoted by Contemplative Outreach and commonly called "Centering Prayer," the sacred word is not repeated like a mantra or slowly beaten like a drum. Rather, it is repeated only when, inevitably distracted by thoughts or feelings, we need a nudge to return to the pure, loving gaze of God; when a distraction grabs our attention, that is when we gently repeat the word interiorly, to "come back" to the conscious awareness of God.

Quality and Fruits

During meditation or contemplation, I am often tempted to analyze or evaluate the prayer experience. "This is great!" or "I must remember how I got here so I can return to this same interior place tomorrow" are self-reflective distractions that say nothing about the quality of my prayer period; such thoughts simply show me I have shifted my attention away from God and onto myself. The quality of my meditation or contemplation is exhibited only in my willingness, when distracted, to keep returning to the pure, loving gaze of God facilitated by the repetition of the mantra or the nudge of the sacred word.

> [T]he fruit of the Spirit is love, joy, peace, patience, kindness, generosity, faithfulness, gentleness, and self-control.
>
> (Galatians 5:22)

The fruits of meditative and contemplative prayer are not experienced during the prayer period. Rather, they are manifested in our daily routine long after the prayer period has come to an end. We find ourselves—usually only in hindsight—glowing with godly enthusiasm and growing in the nine "fruit of the Spirit." This awareness leads us to a deeper appreciation of how the Spirit uses our pure, loving gaze of God to transform us into little Christs: "Lover transformed in the Beloved," to quote the line from John of the Cross's allegorical poem "Ascent to Mount Carmel."

■ REFLECT

1. When have you considered this type of prayer out of reach or inaccessible to you? What do you think now?

2. When have you felt the desire just to bask in God's presence without words or thoughts? What keeps you from doing so?

3. How do you think meditation and contemplation fit into Teresa of Avila's definition of prayer as a frequent heart-to-heart conversation with him by whom we know ourselves to be loved? How can a conversation between you and God occur if words are not used?

■ GO DEEPER

James Finley, *Christian Meditation: Experiencing the Presence of God. A Guide to Contemplation* (San Francisco: HarperSanFrancisco, 2005).

Laurence Freeman, "Meditate with Father Laurence Freeman," http://www.youtube.com/watch?v=zTCFBRF7K0A.

Thomas Keating, "Centering Prayer Guidelines Intro," http://www.youtube.com/watch?v=3IKpFHfNdnE.

Martin Laird, *Into the Silent Land: A Guide to the Christian Practice of Contemplation* (New York: Oxford University Press, 2006).

The Way of Peace, "Christian Meditation," http://www.youtube.com/user/thewayofpeace/featured.

CHAPTER 14

LECTIO DIVINA

∎

On the evening of the second Sunday of every month, about one hundred Catholics in Toronto gather at St. Michael's Cathedral. After the celebration of evening prayer, Thomas Collins, the cardinal archbishop of Toronto, leads the gathered congregation in a forty-five-minute practice of *lectio divina*, the sacred reading of Scripture. Cardinal Collins initiated this devotional practice in his cathedral in response to Pope Benedict XVI's statement in September 2005: "If [lectio divina] is effectively promoted, this practice will bring to the Church—I am convinced of it—a new spiritual springtime."

What Is Lectio Divina?

Lectio divina is the ancient practice of praying with Scripture. Its roots date back as far as the sixth century. It is not "reading" Scripture for information but rather "submitting" to it for transformation. Its basic premise is that God has a burning desire to be in a relationship with us, and Scripture is God's living love letter personally addressed to each one of us. If we allow ourselves to be vulnerable before this living word of love, the Spirit will use the practice of lectio divina to help us catch the fire of godly enthusiasm and mold us into little Christs.

Traditionally, lectio divina has been practiced privately, though nowadays, such as in Toronto's cathedral or, in my case, with a group of five of my friends every week, group practice is gaining popularity. By the late twelfth century, the practice was systematized into the following four steps:

Read. We begin this method of prayer with the slow, attentive, and prayerful reading of a selected Scripture passage. The passage is typically read three or four times to give a sense of the flow and content of the passage. Reading a commentary or the footnotes concerning the passage beforehand can help us understand the selected passage. Some writers like to refer to lectio divina as "feasting on the Word" and compare this first step to taking a bite.

Meditate. The second step of this feast is to "chew" the selected Scripture passage. We reflect upon each word or phrase of this love letter. We ponder its meaning and consider its implications for our own spiritual and moral lives. We brood over the words and mull over how they might be challenging us to change our behavior or attitudes to become more like Christ, or how to respond lovingly to our neighbor. Like any other word spoken in love, Scripture can sometimes be more unsettling than comforting.

Pray. Feasting on Scripture continues with savoring its essence. We engage God in conversation about our thoughts, feelings, and reactions to God's love letter. As the word comes forth from the heart of God, so our prayer arises from the heart. Since prayer is essentially a dialogue, we allow time for God to respond to our prayer of thanksgiving, praise, pardon, petition, or intercession.

Contemplate. The final step of the divine reading is to digest what we have heard and let it become a part of our body and lives. "Let the word of Christ dwell in you richly" (Colossians 3:16). As we allow God to respond to our prayer, we sit in silent, grateful love and bask in God's fiery passion that is revealed in Scripture. Here we willingly submit to the Spirit's transformative process of molding us into the Word made flesh.

Some contemporary spiritual writers like to make explicit a fifth step: *Act*. Having encountered and been nourished by God's love letter, we now continue in the banquet hall of life with new attitudes and behaviors befitting our vocation as little Christs. We have not authentically encountered and submitted to Scripture without a renewed godly enthusiasm or changed behavior.

An Alternative Method

Cardinal Collins of Toronto offers those who attend his monthly lectio divina in the cathedral an alternative way of engaging in this ancient practice of Scripture reading. After a slow, attentive, and prayerful reading of the passage three times, he encourages those present to ask themselves three questions:

What is the passage saying to my head? What does this word say about God's yearning to be in a relationship with me? Scripture gives me knowledge about God and about how God looks upon me as a beloved child. I pause and ponder the divine revelation in the sacred text.

What is the passage saying to my heart? What emotions does this word incite and draw out of me? Though I might feel convicted (and need to change) or even elated by Scripture, nevertheless, I am moved to love and adore this God of unconditional love.

What is the passage saying to my hands? In what ways is this passage calling me to serve God? More than simply a method of prayer, lectio divina also calls me in numerous and varied ways to respond lovingly to the unmet need or required duty of the present moment.

Today, if you hear his voice,
do not harden your hearts.

(Hebrews 4:7)

I have personally found Cardinal Collins's approach to lectio divina helpful in putting on the mind of Christ and following through with action. His three questions highlight Scripture's engagement and influence over my entire being. The practice of divine reading is not just gaining head knowledge, learning where passages are found in the Bible, or even memorizing verses. It goes deeper, allowing Scripture to probe, touch, and move me. My vulnerability and Christlike response show the transformative power of the Spirit and the timeless potential for the Word to become flesh again.

Paintings and Icons

There is a third method of lectio divina that is especially appropriate for prayer that engages religious art, such as paintings and icons. In her second letter to Agnes of Prague, the thirteenth-century Franciscan Clare of Assisi offered some advice about how to look upon the body of Christ on a crucifix. She wrote, "[G]aze [on him], consider [him], contemplate [him], as you desire to imitate him."[14]

We begin by *gazing* upon the figures depicted in the work and their details. We note the expressions on the faces, their gestures, the composition's symmetry or lack of it, the interplay of light and shadows, and other artistic details. After we have studied the portrayal of the scene or person, we *consider* the motivation and intention of the artist: What is the artist saying to us in this depiction? How does the artist convey this meaning? What is striking about this depiction? What is missing or added to the customary depiction of this scene or person? As we ponder the answers to these questions, we find ourselves growing silent as the message of the artwork emerges. This leads us to *contemplation*, where we bask in the artist's visual representation of the scriptural passage or personage. Ideally this concludes with our deeper desire to *imitate* the Christlike qualities or virtues associated with the artwork's message.

The practice of lectio divina reminds us that Scripture and important works of art help us catch the fire of godly enthusiasm and are used by the Spirit to transform us into little Christs.

▪ REFLECT

1. What role do Scripture and religious works of art play in my own prayer life?
2. What does it mean to "submit" to Scripture? How do I know when I am doing this authentically? What makes it difficult?
3. Which method of lectio divina has the greatest potential to touch and transform me?

▪ GO DEEPER

Pope Benedict XVI, "'Lectio Divina' Will Bring to the Church a New Springtime," 16 September 2005, http://www.penitents.org/PBShort.html#_Lectio_Divina_Will_Bring_to_the_Church_a_New_Spiritual_Springtime_.

James Martin, SJ, "Lectio Divina," http://www.youtube.com/watch?v=2DxaGZqprrs.

Christine Valters Paintner, PhD, *Lectio Divina—The Sacred Art: Transforming Words and Images into Heart-Centered Prayer* (Woodstock, VT: Skylight Paths, 2011).

James C. Wilhoit and Evan Howard, *Discovering Lectio Divina: Bringing Scripture into Ordinary Life* (Downers Grove, IL: InterVarsity Press, 2012).

CHAPTER 15

IMAGINATIVE PRAYER

■

I've already mentioned three prayer methods that help us respond to the ardor of God's love and catch fire. There are still others to choose from, practice, and see if you find them helpful. Each in its own unique way helps to facilitate the Spirit's process of transforming us into little Christs sent on a mission of love, mercy, and compassion.

Indeed, the word of God is living and active, sharper than any two-edged sword, piercing until it divides soul from spirit, joints from marrow; it is able to judge the thoughts and intentions of the heart.

(Hebrews 4:12)

One of these methods of prayer uses the mind's eye to harness the power of Scripture. Sometimes called Ignatian contemplation, imaginative prayer, or composition of place, it engages our imagination—our senses, emotions, and intellects—to make us present as Jesus ministers to people in different Gospel narratives. As we enter and experience a particular Gospel scene, the Spirit can ignite the fire of godly enthusiasm.

The Method

This method of prayer has nine basic steps.

1. Begin by choosing a Gospel story. It could focus on someone in need of a

healing, a miracle of Jesus, a question posed by the apostles, or a time when Jesus was alone in prayer.

2. Say a prayer to the Holy Spirit asking for help and guidance as you enter into the scene. Pray for the grace to be open in whatever way the Spirit desires for the sake of your transformation. Pray also for the wisdom and courage to selflessly respond to the promptings of the Spirit during this prayer time.

3. Slowly and meditatively read the Gospel passage two or three times. You want to become familiar with the people involved, the sentiments expressed, and the plot and flow of the story.

4. Once you are familiar with the story, close your eyes, and, using your imagination, "compose the place." Reconstruct the entire scene. Start with the weather and the physical location. What are they like? Consciously consider all five of your senses to fully experience the story. What are the smells and sounds? Picture Jesus. What does he look like, how is he dressed, and what emotions do his actions convey? Picture the disciples and those who follow Jesus. What are they like, and how are they responding? Imagine everyone involved in the plot of this Gospel story and note their actions and reactions.

5. Put yourself in the scene. Where do you find yourself in the story? Are you an idle bystander watching what is happening, or are you an active participant in the story? How are you dressed? How are you reacting and responding? What are your feelings?

6. After you reconstruct the entire scene and have found your place in it, allow the plot to play out. Is it as described in the Gospel passage, or are there twists and turns not found in the Gospel but which your imagination includes? As the plot plays out, note your emotional reactions and intellectual insights. This is the central part of imaginative prayer, so allow as much time as you need with it.

7. Gradually move from the biblical story to your own life. Freely associate the entire Gospel story with your own experience, and notice what the Spirit prompts you to remember, reconsider, or reflect upon. Do the story and plot remind you of anything in your life, past or present? For example, the raising of Lazarus might call you to consider a relationship that you thought was dead in your life but has recently reemerged in a surprising new way. The woman caught in adultery might speak to you of your own infidelities. The story of blind Bartimaeus might tap into your own deep desire to gain a new perspective or to see an event or circumstance in a whole new way.

8. Upon completing the imaginative prayer, ask yourself how you plan on actively responding to this period of prayer. Will you walk away with gratitude, with knowing that you need to seek forgiveness from someone or offer forgiveness to someone, with the challenge of living with greater faith and trust? This is where we need to listen to the promptings of the Spirit and how the Spirit wants to transform our thoughts, feelings, or actions.

9. Conclude this period of time with an appropriate prayer. It might incorporate praise, thanksgiving, petition, forgiveness, or intercession.

Some people like me do not have active imaginations. But we can still mull over the scene and reflect upon how the plot might help us catch the fire of godly enthusiasm in our lives. As Douglas J. Leonhardt, SJ, wisely notes, "Vividness is not a criterion for the effectiveness of this kind of prayer. *Engagement is* and the result is a more interior knowledge of Jesus."[15] And so we engage the story in whatever way we are able.

I have often tried to get in the boat with the disciples and be with them as they are tossed about by the storm at sea (see Matthew 14:22–

33). It's a challenge for me since I don't have an active imagination and I can count on two hands the number of times I've been in a boat in my entire life. Even though nature and experience haven't given me much imaginative and sensory material to work with, I still find great light and warmth in this Gospel passage—it's been my favorite for years! As Jesus comes to the disciples walking on the water and is mistaken to be a ghost, I think back on the many times that I've been in an emotional storm—Dad's suicide, vocational crises, my departure from China as a missionary—and how Jesus came to strengthen me though I initially didn't recognize him. Watching Peter leave the security of the boat and do the impossible by walking on water gets me reminiscing about how I too was called beyond my comfort zone and asked to do what I thought was the seemingly impossible. Jesus's stretching out his hand to a sinking Peter with his admonition, "You of little faith, why did you doubt?" as he brings him back to the boat chides me to always remember that even the thinnest thread of faith can get me through the rough times. This story has often illuminated the dark periods of my life.

A Typical Reservation

Every now and then at one of my spirituality workshops, someone asks me, "If I am using my imagination, then this is all fantasy, correct? How can the Spirit transform me if all of this is just made up in my head?" These are valid and important questions.

As twenty-first-century Christians, we are coming to learn more and more about the powerful influence of the mind on our lives. Our thoughts can have a profound influence on our desires, passions, and actions. God delights in using all our faculties—intellectual, emotional, and sensual—to satisfy the longing to be in a relationship with us. No aspect of our human nature, be it our intellectual insights, our emotions, or our imaginations, is unreachable and hidden from the grace of God.

So, if we believe in God, we also should believe that God can use every part of us—including our imaginations—to help us come to know him better. Imaginative prayer unleashes our creativity and allows the Spirit free rein to touch our lives in a unique way. Through interacting with the stories of Jesus, we can catch the fire that blazes in the heart of every little Christ.

■ REFLECT

1. What Gospel stories might you turn to first? When and how have they been a source of comfort, consolation, or challenge for you in the past?
2. In what areas of your life could imaginative prayer provide a healing balm? A consolation? A challenge? What would be the appropriate Gospel passages to use?
3. How do you currently experience the continuing ministry of Jesus? In what ways is his ministry in the twenty-first century—including in your own life—similar to his ministry in first-century Galilee and Judea?

■ GO DEEPER

Timothy M. Gallagher, *Meditation and Contemplation: An Ignatian Guide to Praying with Scripture* (New York: Crossroad, 2008).

Ignatian Contemplative Prayer: Praying with Our Imaginations, http://onlineministries.creighton.edu/CollaborativeMinistry/Imagination/index.html.

Ignatian Contemplation—Jesuits of the California Province http://
www.jesuitscalifornia.org/page.aspx?pid=890.

CHAPTER 16

WONDER-ING WITH CREATION

■

I remember taking a walk along the beach of Lake Michigan with six-year-old Jackie. She would occasionally stop, push her toes into the wet sand, and wait for the waves to wash over her feet. And then she would giggle. She encouraged me to do the same, but I refused, thinking such playful gestures foolish. A little bit later, she stopped and stared over the lake toward the horizon.

Wanting to continue walking, I impatiently asked her, "Where are you, Jackie?"

"I'm following the angel across the water to heaven," she replied.

I momentarily paused. I looked at Lake Michigan and followed it to the horizon. I didn't see any angel. As a matter of fact, I didn't see anything worth noticing or stopping for. *What is she talking about?* I asked myself.

And then I realized that Jackie still had her God-given sight, and I reflectively and regrettably wondered when I had lost my spiritual vision.

The Footprints of God

One of the unique gifts that Franciscan spirituality offers is a pair of glasses through which we can look at creation as a ladder to God. From the Franciscan perspective, God the Creator has left behind footprints in creation and, when we gaze upon this created masterpiece with the eyes of a child, we can follow those footprints as if walking up the rungs of a ladder into the divine presence. The treasures on earth boldly proclaim the Treasure above. Childlike eyes fixed firmly on earth are gradually lifted up in a spiritual direction toward heaven. With little Jackie, if we maintain or rediscover our ability to wonder at the world around us, we can be led by the angel across Lake Michigan, beyond the horizon, all the way to God.

Awareness and Attention

I think we all once possessed the ability to climb the ladder of creation. But, sadly, as we grew up, most of us lost the wonder of a child. Utility replaced playfulness as we began to see a source of paper instead of a tree to climb. As we "matured," we lost our stride and the ability to walk in the footprints left behind by God, up the ladder of creation into the divine presence. What had once been done naturally must now be done intentionally.

Some years ago, while preaching in northern Michigan, I had a chance encounter with a Catholic Native American named Charlie. He taught me a simple fourfold technique that many have found helpful in once again following the footprints of God with eagerness and enthusiasm.

"Where are you?" Charlie asked.

I was taken aback by this question. But Charlie reminded me that it's the first recorded question of God in the Bible (Genesis 3:9). I also remember it being the very question I asked little Jackie on the beach of Lake Michigan.

"It's an important question," Charlie continued, "because most of us live with a form of amnesia, completely unaware of where we really are. And so we start right here, right now, becoming conscious of where we are."

I wasn't sure what he meant, so I asked him to explain.

"It's really about learning to be in the present moment. And though we hear so much about that, few know how to do it. It's quite simple. Since the senses tell us where we are, we have to practice seeing what we see, smelling the odors around us, feeling what we are holding, tasting what we are eating, and hearing the sounds of the symphony that is playing around us. This is awareness, and it tells us exactly where we are and what we are doing."

Once we become *aware* of the present moment, Charlie said we must then *attend* to it. This is really the practice of deliberate attention to what our senses are registering. In this second step, we intentionally focus upon the object of one of our senses. It's one thing to see the sun setting out of the corner of our eyes; it's a whole different experience to be attentive to today's sun's final bow choreographed by the clouds and birds. It's a common experience to see a bumblebee flit from flower to flower, but how many times have we watched the way it hovers and lands? And how about a mountain spring: do we feel and taste its pristine beauty?

Assessment and Adoration

"After you have become aware of where you are and have attended to the sumptuous banquet of the present moment," Charlie said, "you then reflect upon it and *assess* what it says about God, God's goodness, God's power, and God's presence. Everything in creation points to the Creator just as every sculpture mirrors the soul of the sculptor. In that way, everything, from giraffes to turnips, says something about God and brings us to God.

"So become aware, experience, and think about the present moment before which you stand. Thomas Merton said that a tree gives

Consider the ravens: they neither sow nor reap, they have neither storehouse nor barn, and yet God feeds them. Of how much more value are you than the birds! . . . Consider the lilies, how they grow: they neither toil nor spin; yet I tell you, even Solomon in all his glory was not clothed like one of these. But if God so clothes the grass of the field, which is alive today and tomorrow is thrown into the oven, how much more will he clothe you—you of little faith!

(Luke 12:24, 27–28)

glory to God just by being a tree. If we could take the time to pause, study a tree, and reflect upon it, we could get caught up in its prayer of praise to the Creator. And that would bring us a conscious awareness of God's loving presence.

"And once we come to that conscious awareness," Charlie concluded, "like Moses before the burning bush, we take off our shoes and bow in adoration. After all, God's presence always leads us to prayer."

I instantly saw the wisdom of Charlie's process of awareness, attention, assessment, and adoration. That evening, as I drove to church, I found myself stopped at a traffic light. Out of the corner of my eye, I saw a bald eagle float against the sky. Still mulling over my conversation with Charlie, I turned the radio off and deliberately focused my attention on the bird. I carefully watched the carefree flight of the eagle. And suddenly, as the light turned green and I was on my way, I was moved to gratitude and adoration as I remembered the words of God, "I bore you on eagles' wings and brought you to myself" (Exodus 19:4).

∎ REFLECT

1. When do you experience the childlike characteristics of wonder and awe in your everyday life? Why do you find yourself resisting them?

2. Spend some time right now right where you are, practicing the fourfold technique of awareness, attention, assessment, and adoration. Then ask: What does it teach me about myself and my location? How can I incorporate this spiritual practice into my daily life?

3. Spend time praying the first five verses of Psalm 8. Then ask: When did I last experience the wonder and awe it celebrates?

∎ GO DEEPER

Judy Cannato, *Radical Amazement: Contemplative Lessons from Black Holes, Supernovas, and Other Wonders of the Universe* (Notre Dame, IN: Sorin, 2006).

Steven Chase, *A Field Guide to Nature as Spiritual Practice* (Grand Rapids, MI: Eerdmans, 2011).

Steven Chase, *Nature as Spiritual Practice* (Grand Rapids, MI: Eerdmans, 2011).

William J. Fitzgerald, *One Hundred Cranes: Praying with the Chorus of Creation* (Notre Dame, IN: Forest of Peace Publishing, 1996).

Christine Valters Paintner, *Water, Wind, Earth & Fire: The Christian Practice of Praying with the Elements* (Notre Dame, IN: Sorin, 2010).

CHAPTER 17

PRAYING THE STATIONS
OF THE CROSS

∎

Catching fire and becoming more Christlike demands a radical identification with Jesus. My own Franciscan tradition places a distinctive emphasis upon it. And nowhere do I find that more challenging than in identifying with the sufferings of Jesus in his passion and death.

The Catholic tradition offers an ancient prayer practice that many people including me find helpful in identifying with the sufferings of Christ. It's referred to as making or praying the Stations of the Cross. Let me tell you about a unique twist that my friend Sandra brings to it.

Sandra knows that some parishioners like to pray the Stations of the Cross in the parish church on the Fridays of Lent at 7 PM. She often joins them. She also prays them year-round.

Sandra believes that praying the Stations of the Cross is more than a mere commemoration of Jesus's final hours on earth; it involves entering and experiencing a transformative process of accepting and surrendering to the cross in her own life. Her cross is debilitating arthritis—and the disappointment that her grandchildren are not currently practicing their faith. When Friday arrives, Sandra knows, as she prays the Stations of the Cross, that it's time once again to allow the Holy Spirit to shape and mold her into a little Christ through forgiveness, love, and patience.

A Short History

The Stations of the Cross find their origins in the Holy Land, where pilgrims desired to visit the places made sacred by the presence of Jesus. Around the fifth century, aware that not everyone could visit Jerusalem, an Italian bishop erected a group of connecting chapels that called to mind some important shrines in Jerusalem. One could now follow Christ in his passion without having to travel to Jerusalem.

During the 1400s and 1500s, the Franciscans built upon this idea, constructing small outdoor shrines across Europe that commemorated various "stations" or stopping places along Jerusalem's Via Dolorosa. Having received papal permission to erect such stations in their own churches in the late seventeenth century, by 1831 the Franciscans held the right to promote the erection of fourteen specific stations in any church as long as the parish priest received permission from his local bishop. And then by 1862 every bishop was given the right to erect stations in any church of his diocese without the intervention of a Franciscan.

Sandra's practice of praying the traditional fourteen Stations of the Cross every Friday steeps her in this rich historical tradition. However, she brings to the devotion her own twist, which helps fire her enthusiasm for God. Though this method of prayer traditionally calls us to reflect upon moments in Jesus's final hours, Sandra challenges herself to look at each station in Jesus's life and ask how she sees *herself* reflected in it. In doing this, she again becomes aware that the Spirit wants to transform her into a little Christ. And so the Via Dolorosa of Jesus sends her toward the cross and tomb in her own life.

The Traditional Fourteen Stations and Sandra's Questions

As Sandra meditatively stands before the painting, carving, or image hanging on the walls of the church that depicts a station, she prays and then asks herself different questions. Here are the traditional fourteen stations and the questions she asks:

May I never boast of anything except the cross of our Lord Jesus Christ, by which the world has been crucified to me, and I to the world. . . . From now on, let no one make trouble for me; for I carry the marks of Jesus branded on my body.

(Galatians 6:14, 17)

1. *Jesus is condemned to death.* How do I respond to unjust accusations? How does the emotional need to defend my ego manifest itself in difficult times?

2. *Jesus takes up his cross.* How do I accept the crosses in my life? How can I willingly embrace them and not actively resist them?

3. *Jesus falls the first time.* How do I respond to the weaknesses of my human nature? When and how have frailty and vulnerability been a blessing in the process of my spiritual transformation?

4. *Jesus meets his mother on the way to Golgotha.* How do I endure the sufferings and heartaches of those I cherish and love? How does my compassionate suffering with others express itself?

5. *Simon of Cyrene helps Jesus carry his cross.* When have I reached out a helping hand to others? How do I lighten the burdens of loved ones and strangers?

6. *Veronica wipes the face of Jesus.* Who bears the imprint of Jesus's bloody face in my life? How am I called to wipe away the tears, fears, and frustrations of prisoners, the homeless, delinquent children, marginalized family members and friends?

7. *Jesus falls the second time.* When have weaknesses and struggles pulled me down? How does the Spirit come to my aid in times of sadness and depression?

8. *Jesus meets the women of Jerusalem.* How have I learned compassion in my own moments of passion and suffering? In what ways do my disappointments and suffering influence the way I respond to others?

9. *Jesus falls the third time.* What moments or events in my life do I consider a failure? How did I and do I respond to them without falling into hopelessness and despair?

10. *Jesus is stripped of his garments.* In what ways have I been stripped of my emotional need for self-concern, self-image, self-gratification, and self-preservation? When do I feel painfully exposed to myself and others?

11. *Jesus is nailed to the cross.* How are anguish, affliction, and suffering transforming mc into a little Christ? When have surrender and acceptance freed me from my self-absorbed ego?

12. *Jesus dies on the cross.* Whom do I still need to forgive before I die? How do my everyday desires and daily actions reflect the way I want to die?

13. *Jesus is taken down from the cross.* What lesson has the grief of saying goodbye to a friend or loved one taught me? What does the Mother of Sorrows say to me?

14. *Jesus is laid in the tomb.* Who will come to my funeral and mourn the loss of my physical presence? How do I deal with the reality of my death?

In some churches, Sandra finds a fifteenth station: *Jesus rises from the dead.* This prompts her to ask herself: How have I experienced the Resurrection in my own life? When has the grace of God caught me off guard and totally surprised me?

The Way of the Cross in the Bible

In 2007 Pope Benedict XVI approved for public celebration a new set of stations offered by Pope John Paul II in 1991. Unlike the traditional fourteen stations, only eight of which have a specific mention in the Gospels, each of these has a scriptural reference that we can use for meditation:

1. Jesus in the Garden of Gethsemane: Matthew 26:36–41
2. Jesus is betrayed by Judas and arrested: Mark 14:43–46
3. Jesus is condemned by the Sanhedrin: Luke 22:66–71
4. Jesus is denied by Peter: Matthew 26:69–75
5. Jesus is judged by Pilate: Mark 15:1–5, 15
6. Jesus is scourged and crowned with thorns: John 19:1–3
7. Jesus takes up his cross: John 19:6, 15–17
8. Jesus is helped by Simon to carry his cross: Mark 15:21
9. Jesus meets the women of Jerusalem: Luke 23:27–31
10. Jesus is crucified: Luke 23:33–34
11. Jesus promises his kingdom to the repentant thief: Luke 23:39–43
12. Jesus entrusts Mary and John to each other: John 19:25–27
13. Jesus dies on the cross: Luke 23:44–46
14. Jesus is laid in the tomb: Matthew 27:57–60

In whatever way you do it, the practice of praying the Stations of the Cross can be a reminder that your personal cross, no matter what form it might take and no matter how or when it might appear, is one of many tools that the Spirit of God uses to transform you into a little Christ sent to respond lovingly to the unmet need or required duty set before you. This might give you reason to join St. Paul in boasting about it in your life.

■ REFLECT

1. How would praying the Stations of the Cross help you accept and surrender to personal suffering? How would this prayer method form you into a more compassionate person?
2. What would you name as the cross or crosses in your life today? Why do you name these as "crosses"?
3. Of the fourteen stations, which one moves you the most to pause, pray, and ponder? Why?

■ GO DEEPER

Mary Ford-Grabowsky, *Stations of the Light: Renewing the Ancient Christian Practice of the Via Lucis as a Spiritual Tool for Today* (New York: Image, 2005).

Caryll Houselander, *The Way of the Cross,* Revised Edition (Liguori, MO: Liguori Publications, 2002).

Megan McKenna, *The New Stations of the Cross: The Way of the Cross according to Scripture* (New York: Image, 2003).

Henri Nouwen, with illustrations by Sr. Helen David, *Walk with Jesus: Stations of the Cross* (Maryknoll, NY: Orbis, 1990).

CHAPTER 18

THE LORD'S PRAYER ANEW

■

A while back, I discovered that the Carmelite mystic Teresa of Avila considered the Our Father a source for contemplative prayer; she even suggested that the person who takes an entire hour to pray just one Our Father will be greatly rewarded.[16] I found those statements intriguing especially since I typically pray the Lord's Prayer three times a day—but usually without much attention to what I am saying.

It was then that I took a step back and began to reconsider the meaning and importance of the Lord's Prayer in my spiritual life. I began something new: During my daily hour-long walks, I started to reflect meditatively upon the words of the prayer. Initially I would get through four or five verses of the prayer with each city block. The more I practiced this method of prayer-walking, however, the longer the spaces of silence became between the verses; I was finding more and more nuggets of meaning that were sparking into flame. I now walk an entire city block with just one verse; sometimes I am actively meditating on a particular verse while other times I am simply basking in the warmth of its fire. Though I still haven't spent an entire hour on just one Our Father as Teresa of Avila suggests, I have discovered the light emanating from this prayer: it is truly a summary of the entire Gospel.

What the Prayer Says about God

Our Father

The Lord's Prayer begins with the image of God as Abba, Father. This childlike image emerged early on in Jesus's life; Luke has an adolescent Jesus refer to the temple in Jerusalem as his "Father's house" (Luke 2:49). This image shaped the good news taught in Jesus's parables about God's fiery passion to be in a relationship with us: God's lavish generosity, unconditional love, and eagerness to forgive (see Matthew 6:25–34; 21:28–32; 5:45; Luke 11:5–13; 15:11–32). It was the motivation behind Jesus's table fellowship with sinners and the marginalized. The attitudes embedded in the image of God as Abba became the benchmark for any person burning with the desire to become more Christlike: "Be perfect, therefore, as your heavenly Father is perfect" (Matthew 5:48). That image and what it represents is passed on to us as we enter into an intimate relationship with the God whom the risen Christ called "my Father and your Father" (John 20:17).

Praying to "our" Father reminds us that entering into this relationship with Jesus's Father is entering into a large, extended family. Hence, Jesus challenges us with the "greatest commandment": love of God *and* love of neighbor (Mark 12:29–31). One love complements and completes the other love. It is love of neighbor, and more importantly love of the enemy, that demonstrates our Christlikeness and the fact that we are children of the Father (see John 13:34–35; Matthew 5:44).

In Heaven

The Lord's Prayer makes clear that though God is Father, there is also a mystery about God that we will never understand or comprehend. Indeed, God dwells "in heaven," a reference Jesus pulled from the Jewish Scriptures indicating that nothing can contain the living God (see 1 Kings 8:27). And yet this mysterious, ineffable God "became flesh and lived among us" (John 1:14) in the person of Jesus of Nazareth.

Thy Name

Jewish tradition has consistently reverenced the name of God, because knowing the name is to give evidence of having an experience and relationship with God (see Exodus 3:13–15). To hallow God's name is to acknowledge not only our relationship but also what God has done in our lives: "[F]or the Mighty One has done great things for me, and holy is his name" (Luke 1:49). After the Resurrection, the early Christian community also recognized the importance and intercessory power of the very name of Jesus (see Philippians 2:9–11; Acts 3:6; 4:10–12).

Thy Kingdom Come, Thy Will Be Done

"Thy kingdom come" calls to mind the cornerstone of Jesus's good news: "The time is fulfilled, and the kingdom of God has come near; repent, and believe in the good news" (Mark 1:15). Jesus challenges us to make this kingdom the priority in our lives (see Matthew 6:33) and compares it to small, ordinary things—seed, yeast, a hidden treasure, a pearl, a fisherman's net (see Matthew 13:24–50)—to highlight how it is realized in the simplest and smallest acts of peace, love, or justice.

The realization of God's kingdom and doing the Father's will were virtually synonymous for Jesus. "My food is to do the will of him who sent me and to complete his work" (John 4:34). He made reference to God's will on many occasions (see Matthew 6:10; 7:21; 18:14; Luke 22:42) and noted that our kinship in his family is based not upon blood ties but upon doing the Father's will (see Mark 3:35).

What the Prayer Says about Us

Therefore do not worry, saying, "What will we eat?" or "What will we drink?" or "What will we wear?" . . . [Y]our heavenly Father knows that you need all these things.

(Matthew 6:31–32)

Daily Bread

The central petition of the Lord's Prayer, "Give us this day our daily bread," acknowledges that we are beggars dependent upon the alms of God, the divine almsgiver and Father. It is a call to a worry-free life and a challenge to radical trust.

Forgive Us

We are not only beggars before God. We are also sinners in search of forgiveness for our trespasses. Jesus made clear that the Father takes the initiative to show us mercy and forgiveness like a father running down the road with open arms to welcome home a wayward son, like a woman who anxiously lights a lamp and sweeps her floor in search of a lost coin, like a shepherd who leaves a flock of ninety-nine sheep and goes in search of one lost sheep (Luke 15:1–32). In his own ministry, Jesus exhibited his Father's extraordinary sensitivity to sinners as he called a tax collector to be his disciple (Matthew 9:9–13), invited himself into the home of another tax collector (Luke 19:1–10), allowed a sinful woman to touch his body and wash his feet (Luke 7:36–50), and refused to publicly condemn a woman caught in adultery (John 8:3–11).

As We Forgive

As forgiven sinners, we are called to become beacons of forgiveness: "Be merciful, just as your Father is merciful" (Luke 6:36; see also Mark 11:25). Indeed, Jesus goes as far as making a direct connection between the forgiveness of our neighbor and God's forgiveness: "For if you forgive others their trespasses, your heavenly Father will also forgive you; but if you do not forgive others, neither will your Father forgive your trespasses" (Matthew 6:14–15, see also 5:7; Luke 6:37–38). Withholding forgiveness is a hypocritical form of injustice that makes us loan sharks liable for punishment (see Matthew 18:23–25).

Temptation

Jesus had experience with Satan and spoke about him on occasion (see Matthew 4:1–11; Mark 3:23–26; Luke 11:14–23; John 12:31). Our final petition in the Lord's Prayer, "Lead us not into temptation but deliver us from evil," is an acknowledgment that we need divine help to expose and refuse the conniving schemes of the devil. Sometimes misinterpreted as suggesting God might lead us into temptation, this petition is better understood as meaning, "Father, do not let us be led by ourselves, by others, or by Satan into temptations; be our savior and redeemer when we fail and sin." It reminds us that Jesus, the conqueror of evil, is the one who saves (see Matthew 1:21; John 16:33) and that, as little Christs, we have been empowered with his authority (see Luke 10:17–19).

Now and Forever

The traditional ending of the Lord's Prayer, "For the kingdom and the power and the glory are yours, now and forever," does not come from the mouth of Jesus; it was a later scribal edition to the Gospel of Matthew. However, it boldly attests to the praise and adoration due only to God the Father.

Slowly praying and meditating upon the words of the Lord's Prayer is an excellent way for glimpsing the heart and soul of Jesus and his ministry. This practice also offers us a succinct review of the worldview and lifestyle of any Christian disciple set ablaze for the glory of God.

■ REFLECT

1. In what areas of your life do the words of the Lord's Prayer challenge you on a daily basis? In what practical ways can you respond to that challenge today?

2. What does your reflection upon the words of the Lord's Prayer tell you about God? About yourself?

3. Try spending one hour in slowly praying just one Our Father. What was the experience like? What did it teach you?

■ GO DEEPER

Albert Haase, OFM, *The Lord's Prayer: A Summary of the Entire Gospel* (www.NowYouKnowMedia.com, 2010).

Albert Haase, OFM, *The Lord's Prayer: The Way of the Disciple* (Downers Grove, IL: InterVarsity Press, 2009).

Mark Hart, *The "R" Father: 14 Ways to Respond to the Lord's Prayer* (Frederick, MD: The Word Among Us Press, 2010).

Kenneth W. Stevenson, *The Lord's Prayer: A Text in Tradition* (Minneapolis, MN: Fortress, 2004).

FANNING THE
FLAME

DISCERNMENT

■

*As we begin to catch fire with various methods
of prayer and see the light reflected in loving
service, we come to know more intimately God's
desires for ourselves and the world.*

CHAPTER 19

DISCERNMENT OF SPIRITS

∎

One evening in Las Vegas, after a long, satisfying day of presenting a workshop on the spiritual life, I was overcome with a feeling of exhilaration. A flame momentarily flared up, illuminated my entire life, and I heard myself blurt out, "I was born to teach and preach!"

Have you ever had an experience like that? Have you ever felt that you were doing exactly what you were meant to do? This is a practical way of experiencing God's spark catching fire and the satisfaction that comes in fanning its flame. It also shows that, by God's grace, you are responding to God's personal invitation to be in a relationship with him.

Figuring out that invitation—what the spiritual tradition calls "discernment"—is no easy task. It includes making important decisions as well as understanding the moods and feelings that come over us seemingly out of nowhere. Both can be confusing and are riddled with their own unique challenges, as a spiritual directee of mine recently reminded me.

Dexter faithfully practices the Examen every evening. On Wednesday or Thursday evenings, he also likes to practice lectio divina and imaginative prayer on the upcoming Sunday's second reading and Gospel. He's been quite intentional about his spiritual life for more than three years now. He once told me, "I feel like God is smoothing off all my rough edges and really shaping me into a whole new person. There are times when I just feel like I am on fire with love for God." I told him that it sounded like he was being slowly transformed into a little Christ.

"But there are other times," he admitted, "when I get terribly confused. Something comes over me, and I suddenly lose interest in my spiritual life. I get restless, discouraged, and just want to give up. I'm not sure why that happens or what that's all about. Am I doing something wrong?"

Discernment of Spirits

Dexter, of course, is not doing anything wrong. Rather, he is experiencing the collision of two worlds. In the sixteenth century, Ignatius of Loyola, founder of the Society of Jesus (Jesuits), wrote insightfully about these two worlds and how to distinguish—discern—the difference between them.

According to Ignatius's understanding, spirits influence our spiritual lives. Some are good and some are evil. The good spirits give us consolations. Not to be confused with "feeling good," the consolation of the good spirits is really a generative and creative force that fans godly enthusiasm and gives birth to inspiration, new ideas, and enlivening energy. It lifts us beyond ourselves and our egos and focuses our attention outside ourselves and toward others. We delight in the joys of others and feel the pain of their sorrows. It strengthens our familial and communal bonds with others. Interiorly, it keeps our most important priorities front and center as well as sharpening our vision for the things of God. As a result, the consolation of the good spirits aids us in being God-seekers and God-finders in the ordinary events of our daily lives.

Working in direct opposition to the good spirits are the evil spirits. Ignatius calls their weapon desolation. This is exactly what Dexter was dealing with in those confusing moments of his life. Sometimes confused with "feeling blue," desolation is spiritual rather than emotional. It smothers our godly enthusiasm and makes us want to give up on our spiritual commitments and practices. It turns us in on ourselves, pushing us down the steps into the dark, dank basement of self-preoccupation and negative feelings. It tries to isolate us there as hostages, cutting us off from family, friends, and community. Desolation is a heavy, dark cloud that impedes our vision and confuses us, leaving us feeling hopeless about any future with God.

Responding to the Spirits

Ignatius not only helps us discern the gift of the good spirits and the weapon of the evil spirits, but he also offers us sage advice about how to respond to consolations and desolations.

In moments of consolation, we should express our gratitude to God with prayers of praise and thanksgiving. We should place these moments in the scrapbook of our memories and periodically call them to mind and review them, especially when we later struggle against the desolation of the evil spirits. We should harness consolation's enlivening energy to fan the flames of godly enthusiasm and deepen our commitment to prayer and spiritual practices. We should also use it to stoke our selfless inspiration and willingness to be shaped by the Spirit's transformative process.

Moments of desolation prey upon the fickleness and frailty of our human nature. I sometimes am overwhelmed by feelings of loneliness and dejection that make me question God's abiding presence in my life. At such times Ignatius encourages us to turn to God and seek

Therefore, to keep me from being too elated, a thorn was given me in the flesh, a messenger of Satan to torment me, to keep me from being too elated. Three times I appealed to the Lord about this, that it would leave me, but he said to me, "My grace is sufficient for you, for power is made perfect in weakness." So I will boast all the more gladly of my weaknesses, so that the power of Christ may dwell in me. Therefore I am content with weaknesses, insults, hardships, persecutions, and calamities for the sake of Christ; for whenever I am weak, then I am strong.

(2 Corinthians 12:7–10)

divine assistance, especially from Jesus, who can sympathize with our weakness and identify with our temptations (see Hebrews 4:15). In times of desolation, we must cling to patience; our faith tells us that God will supply us with sufficient grace to endure and emerge from these times. By deliberately seeking out friends and companions, we should intentionally work against desolation's inclination to become self-absorbed and isolated. Though it might go against the mood that overcomes us in times of desolation, it's also helpful to look for those in need and turn our attention toward them. Knowing that the fire of godly enthusiasm purifies and burns away feelings of desolation, Ignatius encourages disciples to increase their spiritual practices in these trying and dark moments. This is also the time to page through and ponder the scrapbook holding the consolations of the past. And though we might seriously consider changing decisions made during those moments of consolation, Ignatius advises that we hold our ground; moments of desolation are not the time for decision-making.

The Spirit's transformative process has its ups and downs. Though the evil spirits try to hijack the process by attacking us with desolate moments, the consolations given by the good spirits help to fan the fire of God's love in our lives and give us encouragement to surrender to the Spirit's action.

■ REFLECT

1. When have you experienced consolation? How would you describe it? How did you initially respond to it?
2. When have you experienced desolation? How would you describe it? How did you initially respond to it?
3. Reflect on the difference between consolation and desolation. How will such knowledge help you to appropriately respond to each in the future?

■ GO DEEPER

Timothy M. Gallagher, omv, *The Discernment of Spirits: An Ignatian Guide for Everyday Living* (New York: Crossroad, 2005).

Timothy M. Gallagher, omv, *Spiritual Consolation: An Ignatian Guide for the Greater Discernment of Spirits* (New York: Crossroad, 2007).

Mark E. Thibodeaux, sj, *God's Voice Within: The Ignatian Way to Discover God's Will* (Chicago: Loyola Press, 2010).

CHAPTER 20

GOD'S WILL AND DECISION MAKING

∎

Ever since I was "knee-high to a duck," as we say in New Orleans, I dreamed of being a missionary to China. I distinctly remember watching the *CBS Evening News* one day as a fifteen-year-old and having that idea glow hot again. On that particular July evening in 1970, Walter Cronkite showed a video clip of Maryknoll Bishop James Walsh walking to freedom as he crossed the Lo Wu Bridge from present-day Guangzhou (then Canton) to Hong Kong. Imprisoned for more than a decade in Shanghai, Bishop Walsh was the last and longest-held foreign clergyman to be released from prison by the Chinese Communist government.

Thirty years later while on a fact-finding mission for the Franciscan Order, I stood on that very bridge in Hong Kong and asked myself, how do I know if God is calling me to walk to the other side as a missionary?

People ask such questions when standing at a personal or professional crossroads and needing to make a decision. Posed with God in mind, the question implies the person wants the decision to be pleasing to God and according to God's plan. In effect, the question arises from the fire of godly enthusiasm—and the desire to do something about it.

God's Will, Our Gift

Many of us mistakenly think that God has a predetermined master blueprint or a detailed script for each individual life. A faithful person has to figure it out, hope to get it right, and then buckle under to obey. However, such a notion smacks of the pagan idea of fate and does not respect human free will as one of the celebrated gifts of God to us.

The New Testament does state that there is a divine will and that it has been revealed: "[God] has made known to us the mystery of his will, according to his good pleasure that he set forth in Christ, as a plan for the fullness of time, to gather up all things in him, things in heaven and things on earth" (Ephesians 1:9–10). To accomplish this, God needs "co-workers for the kingdom of God" (Colossians 4:11) and "ambassadors for Christ" (2 Corinthians 5:20) who, like Christ, will find their nourishment in doing God's will (see John 4:34). In other words, God needs little Christs.

God's urgent longing for us includes the hope and desire that we will be transformed to help with God's long-term plan. As Eugene Peterson paraphrases it, "It's in Christ that we find out who we are and what we are living for. Long before we first heard of Christ and got our hopes up, [God] had his eye on us, had designs on us for glorious living, part of the overall purpose he is working out in everything and everyone" (Ephesians 1:11–12, THE MESSAGE). Our response to God's longing and the divine designs for our glorious living becomes the gift we present back to God.

Discernment

The process of deciding upon that response is what discernment is all about. As the Latin *discernere* suggests, it requires "separating

Do not quench the Spirit. Do not despise the words of prophets, but test everything; hold fast to what is good; abstain from every form of evil.

(1 Thessalonians 5:19 – 22)

off," "distinguishing," and "sifting away." What has to be separated off, distinguished, and sifted away? Our attraction and allegiance to the false self's obsession with self-concern, self-image, self-gratification, and self-preservation. To do so requires openness, self-honesty, courageous generosity, and well-aligned priorities. Once these attitudes are in place, we are then free to make the best decision that will help facilitate our transformation into little Christs, sent to respond to the needs set before us.

There are two principal ways of discerning, their use depending largely on an individual's personality and preference. Some of us think through a decision cerebrally, basing it on reason, good judgment, logic, and common sense. Others, like me, prefer to feel our way to a decision based upon the heart and our gut reaction to a situation. In either case, the time-tested advice for striking a balance is well worth remembering: Thinkers should "trust your head but use your gut," and feelers should "trust your gut but use your head." Discussing upcoming decisions with family, friends, and trusted confidants helps to keep that balance center stage; discerned decisions made in secret can be quite risky.

From personal experience I've learned to give ample consideration to the past, the present, my potential, my passion, and my baptismal identity. Each plays an important role in determining a personal response to God's greater will.

We are all products of our *past*. Our family and home dynamics, the values we were taught and have assimilated, and our educational experiences have left a profound impression on each one of us. Past scars and wounds might have to be addressed before the discernment process can even begin, lest we find ourselves emotionally stuck. Are today's decisions being motivated by old resentments, shames, or fears? Are these decisions more reactive than responsive to parental values or our home situation? The freer we are as we approach the discernment process, the more our response becomes a gift to God.

Our *present circumstances* present us with obligations, commitments, and responsibilities that typically need to be respected and fulfilled both today and tomorrow. Simply walking away from vows, relationships, jobs, and children could be irresponsible and downright sinful. Openness to the future comes by listening to the present moment and not ignoring our commitments to its unmet needs and required duties. Dialogue with others on this point can be extraordinarily helpful.

Our God-given talents and abilities make up our *potential*. They are clear indicators that we always remain diamonds in the rough. These natural gifts and capacities sometimes give us the opportunity to move beyond the limitations placed upon us by our past and present circumstances. They provide the wrapping paper for our unique gift and response to God.

Passion fuels the fire in our lives and sometimes finds expression in our hopes and dreams. It gives us the courage to break through any fear or obstacle keeping us from the transformation by the Spirit, but it can also surreptitiously stoke the false self's obsession with self-concern, self-image, self-gratification, and self-preservation. That's why self-honesty and rightly aligned priorities are crucial when we begin the discernment process. Jesus's advice is well taken: "No one can serve two masters" (Matthew 6:24).

Our *baptismal identity* is a little Christ. That's who we are and who we are called to be. As we decide upon our response and gift to God in the discernment process, we allow the Word of God, especially the New Testament, to be "a lamp to [our] feet and a light for [our] path" (Psalm 119:105). The degree to which we allow ourselves to be challenged by the Scriptures and enlightened by the Church community's interpretation betrays the intensity of our godly enthusiasm. Perhaps more than anything else, our baptismal identity, which includes God's designs for our glorious living, is the woodstove of the discernment process.

My Gift to God

Knowing full well that Lo Wu Bridge was Bishop Walsh's path to freedom, I lingered there for more than two hours as I asked, how do I know if God is calling me to be a missionary in China? That afternoon and over the next few weeks, I recalled my childhood fascination with China and seeing Bishop Walsh walk across this bridge on television. As a Franciscan friar, I knew the Franciscan Order wanted to reestablish its presence in mainland China in whatever way it could, and I believed

I had the skills to learn the language and the passion to understand the culture. Walking across this bridge would give a new dimension to my preaching ministry and my Christian discipleship. My family and friends supported and encouraged my emerging decision. Feeling it was the right choice to make, I began fashioning my response to God's will by putting one foot forward and starting what would become a twelve-year journey as a missionary in mainland China.

■ REFLECT

1. How do you understand the will of God? What do you think are God's designs for using your godly enthusiasm?

2. Whom do you consult when discerning and making an important decision? Why? Which of the five elements of discernment do these people help you to consider?

3. Revisit a past decision that has proven to be unwise. What was faulty in your discernment? What information in this chapter will be helpful to keep in mind in your next discernment?

■ GO DEEPER

Stefan Kiechle, *The Art of Discernment: Making Good Decisions in Your World of Choices* (Notre Dame, IN: Ave Maria Press, 2005).

Elizabeth Liebert, *The Way of Discernment: Spiritual Practices for Decision Making* (Louisville, KY: Westminster John Knox Press, 2008).

Joseph A. Tetlow, SJ, *Making Choices in Christ: The Foundations of Ignatian Spirituality* (Chicago: Loyola Press, 2008).

Pierre Wolff, *Discernment: The Art of Choosing Well Based on Ignatian Spirituality* (Liguori, MO: Liguori/Triumph, 1993).

CHAPTER 21

DRYNESS, DARKNESS, OR DEPRESSION?

■

As we fan the flames of enthusiasm in our lives, with God's help, we encounter three different realities that try to extinguish the fire in our lives. It's important to discern and differentiate these three: dryness in prayer, spiritual darkness, and clinical depression. Each is distinct and requires a different response.

Dryness

Spiritual dryness typically occurs during prayer time and is a temporary feeling of boredom, tedium, disinterest, and monotony. One's prayer is flat, sterile, cold, and uninviting. Saying prayers and reflecting upon God become hard, wearisome, and difficult to maintain. This can last for an entire day's prayer period, for a few days, or even a month or two. It is typically me-centered ("My prayer is meaningless. I'm not getting anything out of it" is the usual complaint) and fleeting, rarely lasting longer than two months.

When experiencing dryness, we often think we are doing something wrong; we think, if I adjust my prayer technique, I could regain my momentum and again find my stride in prayer. Such a misconception is bound to lead to frustration as we try to find that inner place where prayer used to come so easily. Dryness is a perfectly natural experience for anyone who has made the daily commitment to prayer. When we experience it, we are doing nothing wrong.

One of the great paradoxes in the spiritual life is that dryness in prayer is really an indication that something is cooking. It's a sign that the Spirit's transforming process is at work and is calling us to surrender control over our prayer techniques. We are being moved to a simpler form of prayer, one that is not so dependent on saying words or thinking and meditating upon God.

What do we do during periods of spiritual dryness? We keep showing up; we remain faithful to our prayer time. It's easy to forget that simply showing up and going through the motions is a sign of our fidelity—and God blesses it. Rather than forcing words, we can follow the silence and sit with loving attention upon God. Slow and meditative repetition of a prayer word or mantra, in sync with our deliberate breathing, can be helpful in maintaining our loving attention.

Darkness

Unlike dryness, which is me-centered, darkness is God-centered. Specifically, God suddenly seems absent, disinterested, and indifferent to us. This darkness occurs after we have built a history with God and feel confident of his determination to be in a relationship with us.

The Carmelite mystic and doctor of the Church John of the Cross enumerated two "dark nights." (Contrary to popular belief, he never used the term "dark night of the soul.") The first is called the *dark night of the senses* and is characterized by a general and prolonged dryness in prayer along with the fear of being lost on the spiritual journey. We think that some sin or weakness has offended God; we are therefore being punished with God's absence. Some Christians, beset by sexual temptations and trials, wonder why these are so persistent when they keep rejecting them; some are tempted toward blasphemy and blaming God and think that their relationship with God is irrevocably broken;

still others are racked with scruples, vocational doubts, or confusions that challenge their need to feel right with God.

The God-initiated dark night of the senses, painful as it is, involving one's personal limitations, challenges and removes all one's emotional attachments to consolations and feelings of peacefulness, prayerfulness, and joy. It is a call to spiritual poverty as God nudges one not to confuse the gifts with the Giver; this confusion is often what gives rise to the need for the dark night of the senses. It is a call to surrender in faith to the mysterious God who is beyond all emotional feelings, sensibilities, and consolations.

It was now about noon, and darkness came over the whole land until three in the afternoon, while the sun's light failed; and the curtain of the temple was torn in two. Then Jesus, crying with a loud voice, said, "Father, into your hands I commend my spirit." Having said this, he breathed his last.

(Luke 23:44–46)

The second darkness, the *dark night of the spirit*, is undergone by relatively few people. It is a deeper and more profound experience of darkness, God's absence, and one's sinfulness than the dark night of the senses. Enveloped in the dark night of the spirit for fifty years, Mother Teresa of Calcutta's admission to her spiritual director, "The place of God in my soul is blank.—There is no God in me,"[17] speaks directly to it. These people feel quite capable of committing any and every sin and are totally dependent upon God's help to avoid sin—yet God seems gone. They feel more intensely than others a lingering semblance of selfishness and sin; the few who have experienced this night, though looked upon as great saints and mystics by others, are the "worst of sinners" to themselves. During this darkness—the more pro-found of the two types—a person's faith, hope, and love are being radically purified while the person is challenged to live a deeper form of Christ's self-surrender and abandonment. The Spirit is transforming this person into a little Christ who can more closely identify with the Christ of the Garden of Gethsemane and of Calvary.

This second God-initiated darkness is a practical antidote to the most tempting form of idolatry, in which a person confuses one's images of God with the reality of God. In the dark night of the spirit, one is challenged to move beyond the natural human need to feel God's presence in the way our images of God suggest or to have God boxed in by our expectations or ideas. Like the dark night of the senses, it too is a call to spiritual poverty—but the poverty in which a person is stripped of one's beloved, trusted, and time-tested images of God. The person is called to surrender to God, who is ineffable and incompre-hensible mystery.

In these two dark nights, we are challenged to believe that God is still very much present to us—God *cannot but be present*!—but in a way that our feeble senses cannot experience and our human minds cannot comprehend.

Depression

Unlike dryness and darkness, which are essentially spiritual in nature, depression is an emotional disturbance that finds expression in physical symptoms such as the inability to sleep or the need to oversleep; loss of physical appetite or conversely overeating; problems with concentration; lack of interest in friends, relatives, and sex; excessively low energy level; prolonged anger or irritability; reckless behavior sometimes expressed in substance abuse; headaches, chronic pain, and digestive disorders. These physical symptoms are often accompanied by negative thoughts of guilt, self-loathing, worthlessness, and, in its most extreme form, suicidal ideations. People who are experiencing dryness or darkness do not experience these characteristics as symptoms of their spiritual struggles.

In some cases, depression can be genetic or hormonal. However, in many cases, it is our reaction to an unexpected or continuing negative life event, such as financial problems, problems with significant relationships, or marriage stresses such as separation or divorce. And there's loneliness, the memory of childhood trauma or abuse, health issues or chronic physical pain, or any other unexpected event that causes undue emotional stress.

Depression makes it difficult to pray or find any consolation in one's relationship with God. As a matter of fact, depression will sometimes challenge and test one's images of God. So it can look like dryness or spiritual darkness. But this is more a by-product of the nature of depression, especially in the religious person, and not an indication of dryness or darkness per se.

Prolonged depression, unlike the passing "blues" that we all experience on occasion, needs to be treated by a competent clinical professional. Attempts at self-diagnosis and self-medication can often only prolong the emotional pain. Professional help needs to be accompanied by social support (connecting with friends, relatives, and sometimes support groups), working on emotional skills (learning how to express emotions appropriately), lifestyle changes (getting regular rest, exercise, eating healthily, learning how to manage stress, changing negative thought patterns), and sometimes medication. Emotional stability gives us confidence for daily life.

Many of us will encounter dryness, darkness, and depression as we fan the fire of godly enthusiasm in our lives. Knowing how to distinguish between them and respond to each of them facilitates the Spirit's process of transforming us into little Christs.

■ REFLECT

1. When have you experienced dryness in prayer? How did you respond to it? What did it teach you about prayer?
2. How have dark periods in your life affected your relationship with God? How was your relationship with God different after the darkness faded and light returned?
3. How attached are you to your feelings in prayer? How do you pray when prayer doesn't make you feel good?

■ GO DEEPER

James Martin, SJ, "Shadows in Prayer: The Seven D's of the Spiritual Life," http://www.americamagazine.org/content/article .cfm?article_id=10687.

Gerald G. May, *The Dark Night of the Soul: A Psychiatrist Explores the Connection between Darkness and Spiritual Growth* (New York: HarperOne, 2005).

Paul Murray, *I Loved Jesus in the Night: Teresa of Calcutta. A Secret Revealed* (Brewster, MA: Paraclete Press, 2008).

Susan R. Pitchford, *God in the Dark: Suffering and Desire in the Spiritual Life* (Collegeville, MN: Liturgical Press, 2011).

Margaret Silf, *The Other Side of Chaos: Breaking through When Life Is Breaking Down* (Chicago: Loyola Press, 2011).

CHAPTER 22

SPIRITUAL DIRECTION

■

I began feeling the attraction to prayer as a sixteen-year-old. I asked a priest about its meaning and how to respond to it. I started meeting with him about once a month to discuss my life and what was happening spiritually. Over the past four decades, I have continued to meet regularly with someone as I have grown in the conviction that the spiritual life is something that we're not meant to do alone.

People who are serious about fanning the flame of godly enthusiasm in their lives typically find a spiritual companion who agrees to accompany them on the journey. This companion is traditionally called a spiritual director.

The term spiritual *director* is something of a misnomer. The term suggests that the companion takes the lead, directs, and tells you what to do. But that is not the proper or traditional role of the spiritual director. As a matter of fact, seasoned spiritual directors always do more listening than talking.

The Holy Spirit and the Spiritual Companion

If we live by the Spirit, let us also be guided by the Spirit.

(Galatians 5:25)

The Christian tradition has always said that there is only one spiritual director on the spiritual journey: the Holy Spirit. The role of the spiritual companion is to help us get in touch with the Holy Spirit, discern where the Spirit is leading us, and encourage us to follow the promptings of the Spirit with a grateful and generous heart. The spiritual companion neither tells us what to do nor tries to convince us of his or her own approach to the spiritual life. The spiritual companion is simply present to be a witness to the Holy Spirit's promptings and to offer us encouragement—and sometimes guidance in the form of suggestions—so we can fully and freely respond to the transformation by the Spirit.

As a witness and a source of encouragement, the spiritual companion holds us accountable as we name and claim God's grace in our lives. That naming and claiming provides the content of the monthly spiritual direction session and forms the heart of the spiritual direction relationship. Together the two parties reflect on the following questions as they relate to the directee:

- *Who* has God recently been using to speak to me?
- *What* is God doing in my life right now?
- *When* have I recently been asked to take a step in faith?
- *Where* is God calling me?
- *Why* is God inviting me to embrace a certain person or a certain situation?
- *How* am I responding?

The answers to these questions help motivate and give the directee momentum to submit to the Spirit's action. The spiritual companion will sometimes remind the directee of what he or she has already experienced and will encourage him or her to remain faithful when fear or fatigue begins to dampen the Spirit's fire.

A spiritual companion or director can be especially helpful when you are trying to discern God's call and voice. The advantages and benefits of having a spiritual director quickly come to light when you ask whether or not to have a child, accept a transfer to another city, or respond to an employment opportunity. A spiritual director can accompany you through periods of spiritual dryness and help you learn from seasons of grief and loss. A spiritual director can also point out stepping stones through the turbulence caused by transition.

Some people mistakenly confuse a spiritual director with a counselor or a life coach. Each has a specific role. A counselor helps us negotiate the emotional struggles and psychological issues that often arise. A life coach teaches us techniques to maximize our time, talents, and potential. A spiritual director is a witness and source of encouragement as we begin to surrender to the Spirit's action and fan the flame of God's love. Though there might be times when a spiritual director makes suggestions that help someone manage emotional hurdles or make the most of their time and talents, the proper place for the spiritual companion is at our side as we respond to the Spirit's movements.

Personal Qualities of a Good Spiritual Director

What should you look for in a spiritual director? A spiritual director should first and foremost be a good listener. After all, you'll want to be able to trust this person with your deepest experiences and emotions. A companion who is always talking, who is suspicious and critical, or who is always trying to fix a situation is not particularly helpful as a witness and source of encouragement when you are attempting to name and claim God's grace in your life. The director should have a wealth of life experience, especially in terms of the midlife transition, and be a person who evidences prayerful faith well lived. A director who is open to wonder and surprise clearly knows that God's ways are not our ways (see Isaiah 55:8). Finally, the ideal spiritual director has an adequate understanding of the faith and spiritual traditions, is informed by basic psychological principles, and has enough self-awareness to know when he or she is being more of a hindrance than a help along the journey.

Of course, no one perfectly possesses all these qualities, but many people possess a few more than others. A spiritual director doesn't have to be a vowed religious or an ordained member of the clergy; there are many laypeople—from homemakers to businesspeople—who have been trained in the ministry of spiritual direction and who possess many of the characteristics of a good spiritual companion.

Finding a spiritual director can take a little legwork. The first place to inquire is at the local church. Many now have on-staff spiritual directors, people trained to accompany church members. Also consider inquiring at nearby convents, monasteries, retreat houses, or Christian conference centers. Many offer spiritual direction as an outreach to the wider Christian community in their area. A third resource is the free website of Spiritual Directors International at www.sdiworld.org. Clicking the tab "Find a Spiritual Director" will lead you to their "Seek and Find Guide" listing directors in hundreds of cities. The spiritual director's contact phone number and religious denomination are listed. The website of Spiritual Directors International includes important questions to ask any spiritual director during an initial, introductory meeting.

People often wonder if payment is appropriate for spiritual direction. There are two opposing schools of thought on this. One says that spiritual direction is a ministry in the church, and those who have been given and called with this gift should freely offer their services (see Matthew 10:8). Traditionally one has never paid for this ministry. But nowadays, offering a stipend to spiritual directors who have invested their time and money in formal training is not unheard of. How much should you offer? I recommend your own professional hourly wage or what you consider the value of an hour of your own time as a fair donation. The vast majority of spiritual directors would never turn someone down for lack of funds to pay for spiritual direction.

In summary, what are the values and benefits of spiritual direction? It strengthens perseverance in times of spiritual discouragement and provides an avenue to name, claim, and celebrate God's grace. It encourages us to respond freely, graciously, and generously to the promptings of the Spirit as the fire of godly enthusiasm blazes in our lives.

■ REFLECT

1. Which qualities and characteristics of a spiritual director would be the most important in a person accompanying you on the spiritual journey? Why those?

2. What hesitations do you have about talking with a spiritual director? Where do you think these hesitations come from?

3. If asked today, how would you answer the questions of a spiritual director: *Who* has God recently been using to speak to me? *What* is God doing in my life right now? *When* have I recently been asked to take a step in faith? *Where* is God calling me?

■ GO DEEPER

Joseph J. Allen, *Inner Way: Toward a Rebirth of Eastern Christian Spiritual Direction* (Brookline, MA: Holy Cross Orthodox Press, 2005).

David G. Benner, *Spiritual Companions: The Gift of Spiritual Friendship and Direction* (Downers Grove, IL: InterVarsity Press, 2004).

Thomas Dubay, SM, *Seeking Spiritual Direction: How to Grow the Divine Life Within* (Cincinnati, OH: St. Anthony Messenger Press, 1994).

Tilden Edwards, *Spiritual Director, Spiritual Companion: Guide to Tending the Soul* (Mahwah, NJ: Paulist Press, 2001).

"Spiritual Directors International." A search for this organization on www.youtube.com brings up numerous video clips.

CHAPTER 23

SELF-CARE AND WELLNESS

■

A Franciscan friar I knew, now deceased, once used mileage points to upgrade to first class on a flight from Los Angeles to New York. As he relaxed and sipped his glass of Scotch, the flight attendant approached and said, "Father, Mother Teresa of Calcutta is in the back of the plane, and if you don't mind, I would like to invite her to sit in this empty seat next to you."

The friar was suddenly embarrassed at being in first class and lost his taste for the Scotch. He tried his best to convince the flight attendant to leave Mother Teresa alone. Three minutes later, the flight attendant returned with Mother Teresa. "Please, Mother," the flight attendant said to her, "take this seat."

The friar blushed with shame and embarrassment as the glass of Scotch became Exhibit A, proving him guilty of a comfortable life, unbecoming a son of the poor Saint Francis.

"What can I get you to drink, Mother?" the flight attendant asked.

The friar slumped in his seat and wished he could hide the evidence in front of him.

Mother Teresa of Calcutta spied the glass of Scotch in front of the friar and replied, "I'll have a glass of red wine, please. Preferably cabernet sauvignon." And turning to the friar, she said with a twinkle in her eye and a wry smile, "Father, doctors say that red wine is so much better for the heart than what you're drinking!"

Halos and Health

Many people find it difficult to think of Mother Teresa of Calcutta drinking a glass of cabernet sauvignon in first class. That's because we often think of saints as thin, ascetic-types with dark circles under their eyes, who mutter prayers under their breath. Tough and determined with no *joie de vivre*, they surely fast daily and have little toleration for rest, relaxation, or exercise.

That was, in fact, the traditional view of holiness. However, over the centuries as our understanding of physical health, human psychology, and the spiritual life developed, so too did our understanding of what it takes to fan the flame of godly enthusiasm. We now understand halos as coming *with* a healthy lifestyle and not at the expense of it. The spiritual life is primarily *life*—and that means experiencing it in a sensible and well-balanced way.

Blessed Are the Balanced

During my four years of theological training as a priest, I decided to fast twice a week as a way to deepen and grow spiritually. On my fast days, I committed to praying an extra hour instead of taking my daily hour-long walk. I also decided not to check my mailbox or telephone my family and friends on those days.

Within three weeks, I found myself becoming blue as Wednesday and Friday approached. On those two days, I became irritable and cranky and resented hearing laughter coming from the dining room. Hearing my reactions to my self-imposed fast from food, exercise, and companionship, my spiritual director cautioned, "When it comes to the spiritual life, overzealousness is a hindrance, not a help, Albert. Fasting and prayer should be coupled with exercise and community life and not be perceived as being in competition with them. Blessed are the balanced."

Balance is a blessing, indeed. Many of us are challenged to achieve and maintain it. We are tempted to live our lives off kilter, allowing predispositions and attractions—however noble and laudatory they might seem—to control us, neglecting our physical health, ignoring the emotional requirements of being human, sometimes even overemphasizing our relationship with God at the expense of our families and friends. That was my mistake as I thought the spiritual life was in competition with my physical and emotional needs. On life's journey, it's so easy to keep our eyes fixed on heaven above and end up bumping our heads below. It's critical to strike a healthy balance mentally, physically, emotionally, and spiritually.

Mental Stimulation. When I asked ninety-two-year-old Sr. Agnes, a cloistered nun, the secret to staying sharp as a tack, she instantly replied, "The daily crossword puzzle in the newspaper! It's one of the best ways to thank God for what's between our ears."

The brain is a muscle that needs to be exercised. The more we use it, the more we keep it in shape. Besides contemplating the daily crossword puzzle, we can read a novel, learn a foreign language (even if we never intend on using it), go to the movies, see a play, visit a museum, or spend the day at the county fair. All of these are ways to celebrate and use the gift of the mind.

People like Augustine of Hippo, Thomas Aquinas, Bonaventure, and Edith Stein also remind us that following the path of the intellect is not only a good way to exercise and thank God for the gift of the brain; it's also a valid way to holiness. For some people, study is part of the spiritual process used by the Spirit to transform them into little Christs.

Physical Needs. Our physical bodies are also gifts to be reverenced. They require plenty of water, healthy food, adequate sleep, and proper exercise. They also need rest and relaxation. They require regular medical checkups for prevention and, sometimes, medical attention. They often show their appreciation with a delightful sigh during a vacation, time spent vegging in front of the television, or when listening to music.

If the needs of the body are ignored, they often go underground and come out in unhealthy physical ways. Angry outbursts, overeating, drinking too much, high blood pressure, suddenly dozing off, or inappropriate sexual behavior can sometimes be symptoms that the body is in distress. We need to listen to our bodies, because they never lie.

The sixth-century Rule of Saint Benedict highlights how care and respect for the body can aid our spiritual growth. Its balanced spirit is summed up in the classic Benedictine motto, *ora et labora* ("pray and work"). It legislates about six hours of daily manual labor, shows wise consideration for the food offered to sick and senior monks, and notes the importance of sleep, permitting a siesta in the summer if needed. I have often wondered if Mother Teresa of Calcutta knew that chapter 40 even allows for wine!

Heart Rates. By their very nature, emotions need to be expressed. People of godly enthusiasm know full well the importance of laughter, joy, desire, hope, sadness, fear, affection, courage, and anger. Each of these emotions needs to be recognized and expressed in an appropriate and healthy way, which might include:

When Jesus saw her weeping, and the Jews who came with her also weeping, he was greatly disturbed in spirit and deeply moved. . . . Jesus began to weep. So the Jews said, "See how he loved him!"

(John 11:33, 35–36)

- watching the wonder and awe of children at play
- spending intimate time with one's spouse
- writing letters to Congress
- visiting friends and relatives
- expressing gratitude and thanksgiving
- enjoying favorite television shows and movies
- giving ourselves permission to cry
- laughing heartily
- giving anger an appropriate voice
- fostering a healthy self-image by affirming, loving, and respecting oneself

In the past twenty years, contemporary psychology has been reminding us that when it comes to personal success "E.I." (Emotional Intelligence) is just as important, and maybe more so, as "I.Q." Remember, the heart rates!

High-strung by temperament, I found myself becoming emotionally disengaged within five months of arriving in mainland China. I was lonely, had lost my appetite, and was having trouble sleeping. I was also developing a distain for everything Chinese. One of the most embarrassing moments of my life occurred when, in a moment of frustration while trying to get a haircut, I blurted out, "Why doesn't anyone speak English around here?" Had I forgotten that I was in the middle of China?

That afternoon, I tried to pray in chapel and couldn't. What's going on inside of me?, I asked myself. I painfully admitted that perhaps I had made a mistake by becoming a missionary. As I reflected upon my feelings and pondered their physical manifestations, I came to the realization that I was in the throes of culture shock. The answer to my question then became kindling for my prayer to God. "O God, have I made a mistake by coming here? I'm struggling. Here's the deal: I'll stay as long as you provide me with the grace of your strength." Attention to my feelings gave me my daily prayer as a missionary to China for twelve years.

The twelfth-century reformer of the Benedictine Order, Bernard of Clairvaux, stressed the spiritual role of emotions and affections. His emphasis highly influenced my own Franciscan tradition. Asking oneself, what am I feeling?, is a great way to foster self-awareness and begin any heart-to-heart conversation with God and others.

Spiritual Desires. It's easy to overlook, think unimportant, or postpone satisfying the needs of our spirits. "I'm too busy to pray today," we often say to ourselves. But satisfying these hungers is also critical for our overall self-care and wellness. Responding daily to our spiritual desires through prayer and spiritual practices, even for ten or fifteen minutes, helps to fan the fire that the Spirit has sparked.

The mind, body, heart, and spirit are like different kinds of wood, each contributing to the burn time and intensity of a fire. Sparked by the Spirit, they ignite into the fire of godly enthusiasm and, if given our due attention, keep that fire burning both day and night.

■ REFLECT

1. Whom do you consider to be holy or saintly? What do their characteristics say about your understanding of holiness?

2. On a scale of one (dangerously off kilter) to five (balanced), how would you rate your awareness of and attention to your mind, body, heart, and spirit? Why?

3. Between your mind, body, heart, and spirit, what do you find the most difficult to be attentive to? Why?

■ GO DEEPER

Eugene T. Gendlin, *Focusing*, 2nd (Revised) Edition (New York: Bantam, 1982).

Daniel Goleman, *Emotional Intelligence: Why It Can Matter More Than I.Q.* (New York: Bantam, 1997).

Jeremy Langford, *Seeds of Faith: Practices to Grow a Healthy Spiritual Life* (Brewster, MA: Paraclete Press, 2007).

James Martin, sj, *Between Heaven and Mirth: Why Joy, Humor and Laughter Are at the Heart of the Spiritual Life* (New York: HarperOne, 2011).

Robert J. Wicks, *Bounce: Living the Resilient Life* (New York: Oxford University Press, 2009).

CHAPTER 24

DEVELOPING A RULE OF LIFE

■

Joan first heard the suggestion of writing her own rule of life from a parish priest's homily. He noted that some of the great founders of religious communities—Augustine, Basil, Benedict, Francis, and Clare of Assisi—had proposed rules to their followers as a way of becoming more like Christ. He then suggested that writing a personal rule of life could serve as an encouragement and reminder of the commitments one makes to fan godly enthusiasm into flame.

Joan's curiosity was piqued. "But I have to be honest," she added in a spiritual direction session with me, "the idea of obeying an elaborate rule in my life—written by me or someone else—is a little unsettling and unrealistic."

To set Joan's mind at ease, I thought I would explain to her what a rule of life is and isn't.

The Characteristics of a Rule of Life

A rule of life is a statement about how we will be open to and help foster the process of being transformed by the Spirit of God. Specifically, it provides a structure for our approach to CPR (community, prayer, and repentance). It also expresses our commitment to the three primary relationships in our lives: God, others, and self. It proposes a manner of living that reflects our growing love for God, others, and self while respecting our own unique individuality. Far from being an elaborate and meticulous ordinance requiring dotted *i*'s and crossed *t*'s, a rule of life is more like a gardener's trellis that supports a living vine and helps it grow. It offers a rhythm for living life to the full and being open to the Spirit.

A rule of life is not an ideal we are striving to achieve, written from the shoulds and oughts of a guilty conscience, but rather the minimum standard of our lived experience. "There are certain things I do and just don't do because I am in a committed relationship." This kind of thinking provides the content for a realistic statement of your present circumstance and sets the benchmark for your relationships with God, others, and self for which you can honestly and truly be held accountable.

In its nuts and bolts, simply put, a rule of life is a written document. It can be of almost any length, but I find that the most effective ones fit on one page.

Every person's rule will be uniquely phrased, depending on his or her personality and life situation. The rule is meant to express your answers to some specific questions: How am I personally committed to God? In what ways? What is my unique role in the world—how will I be open to the Spirit and fan the fire of godly enthusiasm in my life?

The most realistic rules are not written in one sitting; they are written, rewritten, and tweaked over days, weeks, and months until they truly express how we are living and want to live as little Christs. They are living documents that, if kept in our journal, indicate how we have changed and grown in each season of life.

Before beginning to write a rule of life, it is worthwhile to ponder and pray over the following questions:

• When and where do I feel closest to God? How do I enter most deeply into a contemplative awareness of God's presence in my ordinary life? What, if any, particular practices are more helpful for me to become a God-seeker and God-finder? What spiritual practices of community life, prayer, and/or repentance (CPR) weigh me down or slow me down on the spiritual journey?

• What is most important to me? What do I really want out of life, and what's stopping me from getting it? Looking at my calendar and checkbook, who or what receives the most attention in my life? If I had only six months to live, how would I spend my time and money?

• When I reflect upon my relationships with God, others, and myself, how do I answer the following questions: What do I want to start doing? What do I want to stop doing? What do I want to do with greater deliberateness and intentionality?

• How do I currently realize my goals and longings for work? For studying? For praying? For relating to significant others and friends? For networking with colleagues? For maintaining diet and exercise? For playing and recreating? Which of these activities foster or dampen the fire of godly enthusiasm for me? Which need greater attention?

• In light of the limitations in my life right now—my interior longings as well as my external responsibilities, what spiritual, relational, and educational practices suit my daily, monthly, and yearly rhythms?

• What can I change in my life? What am I powerless to change?

A Possible Structure for Your Rule of Life

When he came to Nazareth, where he had been brought up, he went to the synagogue on the Sabbath day, as was his custom. He stood up to read, and the scroll of the prophet Isaiah was given to him. He unrolled the scroll and found the place where it was written:
"The Spirit of the Lord is upon me,
  because he has anointed me
to bring good news to the poor.
He has sent me to proclaim release to the captives
  and recovery of sight to the blind,
to let the oppressed go free,

After spending significant time reflecting and working through these questions, you can begin building the trellis that will become your rule of life. It's important to remember that the language used and the structure adopted are just two creative considerations that make the rule of life uniquely yours. Here's one possible structure:

- *Life Statement*: A short, concise one-sentence summary of your personal spirituality. Think of it as a twenty-second elevator speech in answer to the question, "Why did God create you?" This could be a passage from Scripture, a personal mission statement, or some phrase or expression that you gravitate toward because it sums up the ideals you strive for in your relationship with God, others, and self.

- *Preamble*: A brief three- to four-sentence explanation of your life statement. Why is your life statement important to you? What are its practical implications in your daily life?

- *Your Relationships*: Write one or two sentences about the importance of

to proclaim the year of
the Lord's favor."
And he rolled up the
scroll, gave it back
to the attendant, and
sat down. . . . Then he
began to say to them,
"Today this scripture has
been fulfilled in your
hearing."

(Luke 4:16–21)

each of your key relationships: with God, others (your significant other, your family, your wider circle of friends, your colleagues at work, and the family of creation), and yourself. If you were on your deathbed, what would you want to say to each if given the opportunity?

- *Your Commitments*: State clearly and explicitly what you will do to foster and celebrate each relationship (God, others, and self) on a daily, weekly, monthly, and yearly basis.

- *Accountability*: How will you hold yourself accountable to this rule of life? How often will you revisit it to check it, tweak it, and make sure it continues to be a living document? With whom will you be sharing it (spouse, trusted friend, spiritual director, etc.)?

An Example

Adam, forty years old, is married with two children and works as an administrator in a hospital. With his gracious permission, I share with you his rule of life, which sits in a frame on his desk at work:

As a disciple of Jesus Christ, I am committed to living out the teachings of Jesus. As a husband, I am called to make the Father's love a reality for my wife. As a father, I am committed to supporting my wife in raising our children. As a colleague and friend to many, I will live the Golden Rule both professionally and personally.

- *Discipleship: I am committed to twenty minutes of solitary prayer a day and to weekly church attendance with my family. Three times a month, I spend time meditating on Scripture and/or reading a spiritual book. Every June, I attend a weekend retreat (two overnights) with the men's club of my church.*

- *Husband: I will reverence and celebrate Laura as God's love made flesh for me. I am committed to a daily phone call to her from work, a weekly date night, and an annual vacation with her and the children. We are open, honest, and follow Ephesians 4:26-27.*

- *Father: As gifts from God, my children come before my career. I support Laura in her decisions about them and will not drive a wedge between her and them. Twice a month, I spend quality time with each one of them individually and will do my best to offer them memorable annual vacations.*

- *Colleague and Friend: I live by the Golden Rule with no exceptions. When warranted, I treat a colleague as a friend. I stay in touch with my three closest friends on a monthly basis and when possible, invite one for coffee once a month.*

- *Myself: I commit to some form of physical exercise three times a week. I also commit to splurging on myself in some way, shape, or form three times a month.*

I will share this rule with Laura. Every September, I will revisit it, revise it if necessary, and recommit to it.

In summary, a realistic rule is born from reflection upon one's present life and addresses how to create and promote a balanced, healthy lifestyle. Many people initially write a rule that is top heavy in one relationship while ignoring or neglecting others. That's why we need to rewrite and tweak it over time, making sure we are promoting a healthy interaction and balance between being/doing, prayer/action, engagement/solitude, words/silence, speaking/listening, asceticism/celebration, and body/spirit. The process of spiritual transformation that the Spirit accomplishes in us begins *right where we are* in *this* life, not another.

Second, a realistic rule of life is not a rambling litany of overcommitments or unmet ideals longing to be fulfilled. It states a person's current *lived* reality and should fit on one typed page. State what is doable and can be measured with specific, observable behaviors. A rule of life is not a straitjacket that binds but a passport to freedom, creativity, and new adventures.

As we grow in Christ, we will come to view our rule of life as a mission statement that not only proclaims the grace of God in our lives but also gives us direction in setting the world on fire.

■ REFLECT

1. What do you find most challenging about writing a rule of life for yourself?

2. What difference would it make to actually write down your commitments to God, others, and self and then share them with your spouse, best friend, or spiritual director?

3. What relationships in your life do you simply let happen and not intentionally foster and promote? How would a rule of life actively strengthen awareness of those relationships?

■ GO DEEPER

Margaret Guenther, "Creating a Rule of Life," http://www.youtube
.com/watch?v=gmfSfkYPLrM&feature=related.

Laurie Beth Jones, *The Path: Creating Your Mission Statement for
Work and for Life* (New York: Hyperion, 1996).

Stephen A. Macchia, *Crafting a Rule of Life: An Invitation to the Well-
Ordered Way* (Downers Grove, IL: InterVarsity Press, 2012).

TheSpiritofLife.org.uk, "Rule of Life.mpg," http://www.youtube.com
/watch?v=_lpFPrZy2Sk&feature=player_embedded.

BECOMING ALL
FLAME

DYNAMIC COMMITMENTS

■

The Spirit of God energizes us with vigor and passion that keeps the fire of godly enthusiasm blazing in our lives.

CHAPTER 25

AN EXAMINATION OF CONSCIENCE

∎

God's spark catches fire in the lives of many people. You can feel its warmth in those kneeling in Eucharistic adoration chapels, serving in soup kitchens, offering loose change to beggars on the street, silently praying as they commute to work, and selflessly sacrificing for their children. That fire is fanned when these people take responsibility for their spiritual transformation by opening themselves to God's will, spiritual direction, a healthy lifestyle, and being accountable for living an intentional life of faith.

But the fire of godly enthusiasm doesn't stop there. It blazes in commitments that foster and fuel the spiritual practices I have already discussed. These commitments possess a dynamism that will serve as an important reminder: you are not only called to catch fire and become a little Christ but you are, in fact, designed to become all flame!

My friend Martha told me about her experience with one of those dynamic commitments, a weekend retreat.

During his first session on Friday evening, the preacher asked the forty people on retreat a simple question, "How are you doing with God?" He then began to walk them through the Ten Commandments and the Beatitudes of Jesus, asking questions after each one: "I am the Lord, your God. You shall not have strange gods before me. *What are the strange gods that I worship in life? Money? Food? Sex? My reputation?* . . . Blessed are the meek; they will inherit the earth.

How have I abused the power and authority entrusted to me by my vocation in life, my occupation, and the roles I play at home or in the community? How can I grow in the childlikeness and humility that Jesus shows to be important in the kingdom of God?"

That first session gave Martha the impetus to go to confession—something she hadn't done in a very long time. It also introduced her to a simple method of self-reflection recommended to those who respond to the spark from God, fan godly enthusiasm in their lives, and then stoke its flame to keep it burning.

The Importance of Self-Reflection

To be shaped by the Spirit into little Christs, we need to become aware of the rough edges in our lives, those places where we deliberately choose to live in the darkness and selfishness of sin. Self-reflection and repentance are early and critical tasks in the Spirit's transformative process. Without the awareness of our sinfulness, we risk sabotaging the work of the Spirit.

Over the centuries, self-reflection has been promoted through the practice of an examination of conscience. Unlike the examination of consciousness ("Examen") mentioned in chapter 12, the examination of conscience is the deliberate review and analysis of our thoughts, words, and deeds—and, more importantly, their motivations—in the light of our response to God. We sift through them in a measured, meticulous, and methodical way, to be aware of the control that the false self continues to yield over our minds and hearts. The result of such an examination is the deliberate decision to add more kindling to the fire of our godly enthusiasm.

There are numerous ways to examine one's conscience. The retreat preacher had introduced Martha to two common forms: one

Happy are those who do
not blunder with their
lips,
and need not suffer
remorse for sin.
Happy are those whose
hearts do not condemn
them,
and who have not given
up their hope.

(Sirach 14:1–2)

based on the Ten Commandments and one based on the Beatitudes. Another method involves reflection on the theological virtues of faith, hope, and charity. You'll find online versions of these three methods in the "Go Deeper" section at the end of this chapter.

The Fruit of the Spirit

In the letter to the Galatians, Paul encourages us to "live by the Spirit" (5:16) and later adds, "If we live by the Spirit, let us also be guided by the Spirit" (5:25). He explicitly notes the nine "fruit of the Spirit" that are practical indications that we are living and guided by the Spirit: "love, joy, peace, patience, kindness, generosity, faithfulness, gentleness, and self-control" (5:22).

If our enthusiasm is fueled by the Spirit of God, then it's wise to ask ourselves how we obstruct, impede, and thwart the Spirit from bringing forth the divine fruit in our lives. Consequently, an examination of conscience based upon the Pauline fruit proves worthwhile and can look like this:

- *Love.* How have the wounds and grudges that I hold on to hindered me from becoming a person of love and acceptance of others, especially those who have wronged or betrayed me? In what ways have I made people pay for my attention and affection? How have I deliberately subverted the practice of the Golden Rule?

- *Joy.* How have I disrespected the gift of life and the wonders of creation that God has graciously bestowed upon me and allowed me to experience? How have my actions and attitudes sabotaged the exuberance for life and the firmly grounded hope that are rooted in the ultimate victory of Christ's resurrection? In what areas of my life have I insulted God with my worries and anxieties?

- *Peace.* How have I passively supported or actively promoted the violence that arises from apathy, prejudice, sexism, and discrimination? When and why have I refused to stand up and speak out for peace and justice? What has caused me distress and restlessness, and why have I continued to yield to it?

- *Patience.* In what areas of my life have I continued to support the false self's knee-jerk reaction to anger? When have I continued to fight against the things I cannot change or refused to accept the inconvenience that is part of daily life? Where have I given up on the desire and willingness to persevere, persist, and promote my relationships with God, others, and self?

- *Kindness.* How have I continued to focus upon myself, my wants, and my desires to the exclusion of others? What has hindered me from being compassionate, helpful, generous, and caring? Who have I continued to treat cruelly, heartlessly, and mercilessly, and why have I done this?

- *Generosity.* How have I continued to be a stingy and selfish person? When and why have I chosen to ignore the poor, the marginalized, and the needy? In what areas of my life have I continued to be self-absorbed, self-obsessed, and self-seeking?

- *Faithfulness.* How have I continued to betray a spouse, a relative, a friend, or a coworker? Where have I found myself slacking off in loyalty and dedication to public commitments? How have I allowed fear and anxiety to paralyze me and threaten me from living a life "full of faith"?

- *Gentleness.* What fear techniques have I used to ensure that I get my way? How have I pulled strings behind the scene and manipulated situations to make sure that I remain in control? To whom and why have I been blunt, discourteous, brash, and brusque?

- *Self-control.* When have I freely given rein to hedonistic desires and fleeting desires? What tempting and sinful situations have I given myself permission to enter? Where in my life have self-mastery and interior freedom been overcome by bondage and slavery?

A commitment to some form of an examination of conscience is critical for anyone who is serious about becoming a little Christ. Far from stirring up shame and guilt, its goal is the awareness of how our deliberate actions, habits, routines, and thoughts throw cold water on and even extinguish the fire of godly enthusiasm. Such an awareness can be brought to the Sacrament of Reconciliation, helps to free us from the false self, and facilitates the transformation by the Holy Spirit.

■ PRACTICE

Spend twenty minutes practicing an examination of conscience. The examination could be based upon the Pauline fruit found in Galatians or upon one of the other three versions found in the "Go Deeper" section of this chapter.

Spend time writing out this examination of conscience. Commit to sharing the personal insights you discovered with your spiritual director.

■ GO DEEPER

Cindy Caliguire, *Soul Searching (Soul Care Resources)* (Downers Grove, IL: IVP Connect, 2008).

Bill Shore, *The Light of Conscience: How a Simple Act Can Change Your Life* (New York: Random House Trade Paperbacks, 2005).

Louis Tronson, *Examination of Conscience upon Special Subjects* (Charleston, SC: BiblioBazaar, 2009).

Online versions of the examination of conscience:

http://www.scborromeo.org/confess.htm

http://cadyly.stblogs.com/2008/04/15/a-new-examination-of-conscience/

http://www.ewtn.com/library/spirit/examcons.txt

CHAPTER 26

THE CHALLENGE OF FORGIVENESS

∎

Gilbert went through an ugly divorce five years ago. Whenever he has to talk to his ex-wife about their three children, his blood pressure goes up and he lashes out combatively. After those conversations, he finds himself stoking the fires of resentment and reliving the entire divorce. The pain continues even after five years. Gilbert has not forgiven his ex-wife and doubts if he ever will.

The simple truth is this: you can never fully enter into your identity in Christ if you resist forgiving someone in your life.

The Decision

Jesus challenged the understanding of justice found in first-century Judaism. According to the Book of Exodus, justice was rendered by receiving an equitable compensation that balanced the scales of the wrong committed: "eye for eye, tooth for tooth" (21:24). Jesus, however, took exception to this. For him, there is only one form of just compensation, and it is *given* to the accused, not received by the accuser, because we ourselves have already been granted it by God: forgiveness. As the letter to the Colossians succinctly sums it up, "Just as the Lord has forgiven you, so you also must forgive" (3:13).

This form of countercultural justice is a decision, an act of the will. It is also a direct call to die to the false self and its need to find some way to get a petty form of revenge, to feel right and justified. It is not dependent upon an apology; some people, such as the sinful woman who washed Jesus's feet with her tears, have never learned the social grace of directly saying "I'm sorry" and asking for forgiveness (see Luke 7:36–50). And Christian forgiveness does not wait to find some emotional space where it feels good to offer it; Jesus himself forgave his persecutors in the very midst of his betrayal even as he hung upon the cross (see Luke 23:34). Forgiveness is the limitless *choice* not to pick the scab, not to become entangled in the grudge, not to stoke the fires of anger and resentment by hugging the hurt or announcing it to others (see Matthew 18:22).

We often hug the hurt and pick the scab because it makes us feel powerful and intellectually right. We fail to remember, however, that keeping a grudge alive takes a lot of emotional energy. The more we invest in the grudge, the more we are sapped of our emotional stamina. Bitterness, anger, and self-pity become our evening cocktails, as we surrender our serenity and inner peace; they help to continue the betrayal or hurt that occurred weeks, months, or even years ago.

Ultimately, if we don't want to commit to forgiveness in imitation of Christ, then we might want to consider forgiving because it's the best thing we can do for *ourselves*! It sets us free and closes the door on the past. Consequently, as the Mayo Clinic's website reminds us, compared with people who harbor grudges, those who forgive have healthier relationships, greater spiritual and psychological well-being, less anxiety and stress, lower blood pressure, fewer symptoms of depression, and a lower risk of alcohol and substance abuse. No other decision in our lives has such ability and power.

The Mechanics of Forgiveness

I was hurt and angry when I was fired at the age of fifty-four. It was the first time I had ever experienced such a thing. Though the newly hired boss of the spiritual direction center used the polite language of "letting you go for financial reasons," I knew she was firing me because of my challenges to her competence as a professional and to the new direction she was giving to the center. Though I told the boss I would pack up and be out of my office within two weeks, I was actually gone within forty-eight hours. I still remember walking out of the office for the last time and muttering under my breath, "Good riddance."

Over the days that followed, I was obsessed with telling anyone who would listen about what had happened. And with each retelling, I would seethe and stoke the fire of resentment.

Within one month, I became more and more uncomfortable sitting so close to the campfire of anger. I knew I needed to move on, and that would only happen with forgiveness.

Familiar with the expression, "Forgive and forget," I thought my future included erasing the incident from my memory. That proved impossible—and a violation of my self-respect. I was surprised when my spiritual director reminded me that forgiveness begins with remembering, not forgetting. I had to walk through the memory of the hurt and relive the event. I had to honestly admit to myself the emotional effects and personal consequences of this perceived betrayal. Without my doing that, forgiveness indeed would be a violation of myself.

My spiritual director then suggested that I take the challenging and empathic step of compassion: "Put yourself in the shoes of the boss and be as objective as you can." Why did she fire me? Did she intend to hurt me or was I overreacting? How did my actions and attitude contribute to the event? Was something else going on in her professional or personal life? As I tried to be as objective as possible and reflected upon these questions, I realized that as the new boss, Martha was trying to prove herself professionally and had the right to choose her own staff and run the center in the way she deemed fit. I also recognized how my brusque actions and judgmental attitude contributed to my firing. This step of compassion, as my spiritual director said, is a vivid reminder that words and actions sometimes say more about the offender than they say about the offended; and sometimes they speak volumes about the offended. Both were true in my case.

You have heard that it was said, "You shall love your neighbor and hate your enemy." But I say to you, Love your enemies and pray for those who persecute you, so that you may be children of your Father in heaven; for he makes his sun rise on the evil and on the good, and sends rain on the righteous and on the unrighteous. For if you love those who love you, what reward do you have? Do not even the tax collectors do the same?

(Matthew 5:43–46)

Forgiveness in no way condones the hurtful or offending action. That's why it is sometimes necessary—especially in cases of verbal or physical abuse—to develop self-protection strategies so we are not in harm's way again. Having said that, little Christs never allow these strategies to completely shut out the betrayer from their hearts. It takes some finesse to develop self-protection strategies and still be faithful to Jesus's challenge to love the enemy.

I previously made the point that forgiveness is a decision. And that decision is the heart and soul of the mechanics of forgiveness. We choose to offer forgiveness as a selfless gift with no strings attached. And in the case of the deepest wounds and most flagrant of betrayals, we typically have to commit to giving this gift again and again, even daily—and especially when we are tempted to take it back.

Six months after being fired, I ran into a former colleague of mine from the spiritual direction center. When he made reference to my absence at the center, I was tempted to rehash my experience of being fired. But I reminded myself that I had forgiven Martha and had moved on. I remember saying to myself again, I have forgiven her and I am choosing to leave the past in the past.

The daily recommitment to this gift-giving shows the stuff of our soul and the intention of our heart. Even though the gift might simply lie in our heads as it did initially in my case, over time we will find it gradually making its way down to our hearts, where it loosens resentment and frees us from the past.

If, for whatever reason, we cannot offer forgiveness, it's helpful to ask, "What am I gaining by stoking the fire of resentment?" An honest answer typically reveals some kind of kickback that satisfies the false self. Perhaps it is the self-righteous need to feel justified and vindicated; perhaps it is some emotional issue from childhood that continues to play itself out. As we pray and reflect upon that question, we might gain further insight if we talk about the issues with a counselor or spiritual director. That helped me. Realize too that no one has ever arrived at the end of life and said, "I'm glad to have stayed angry and bitter for so long."

The Spirit tries to mold our hearts according to the pattern of Jesus's forgiving, merciful, and compassionate heart. We can facilitate this transformation by remembering past hurts, empathizing with our betrayer, choosing to forgive, and recommitting daily to that decision. That choice breaks the stranglehold of the past and gives us the freedom to enjoy life in the present.

■ PRACTICE

Find a place that offers the luxury of time and solitude; it could be in your home, at a park, or in a church. Once settled in a comfortable position, ask yourself, "Whom do I need to forgive? Why?" Once you have identified a person, begin the decision to forgive by walking through the steps:

- Recall the incidents of betrayal or hurt.
- Put yourself in the other person's shoes and try to empathize with their hurtful word or action.
- Make the decision to forgive the person.
- Recommit to that decision on a daily basis until your heart softens and you are set free from the grudge.

■ GO DEEPER

Alice Camille and Paul Boudreau, *The Forgiveness Book: A Catholic Approach* (Chicago: Acta Publications, 2008).

Martin Doblmeier, *The Power of Forgiveness*, DVD (New York: First Run Features, 2007), www.firstrunfeatures.com.

Vince Dipersio, *The Big Question: A Film about Forgiveness*, DVD distributed by Vision Video (Worcester, PA: Vision Video, 2007), www.visionvideo.com.

Robert D. Enright, PhD, *Forgiveness Is a Choice: A Step-by-Step Process for Resolving Anger and Restoring Hope* (Washington, DC: American Psychological Association, 2001).

CHAPTER 27

RESISTING TEMPTATIONS

■

There are other serious and intentional commitments we must make if we want to truly and completely become the little Christ we are called to become. As we submit to the transformative process of the Holy Spirit, we quickly experience temptations by the devil that try to steer us away. We don't hear much about these temptations nowadays—but it is quite advantageous to discuss them. This is an essential topic for everyone who desires to put on the mind of Christ.

The Eight Tempting Thoughts

These temptations were enumerated by the fourth-century Christians who lived in the deserts of Egypt and Palestine. The desert fathers and mothers pinpointed eight thoughts that the devil uses to coax Christians into committing the seven deadly sins. They are thoughts toward pride, greed, anger, lust, gluttony, listlessness, vainglory, and dejection.

These thoughts fuel the four preoccupations of the false self: self-concern, self-image, self-gratification, and self-preservation. The desert monks discovered that entertaining these thoughts or giving them serious consideration weakens our resolve to resist them. That's why the monks thought it imperative to be aware of the insidious nature of these temptations and to learn how to confront them immediately.

To resist the devil's tempting thoughts, the desert fathers and mothers employed a technique called "talking back," reciting and repeating memorized Scripture as a method of defense. This technique would "cut off," to use the expression of the desert monks, the corresponding temptation.

Then the devil took him to Jerusalem, and placed him on the pinnacle of the temple, saying to him, "If you are the Son of God, throw yourself down from here, for it is written, 'He will command his angels concerning you, to protect you,' and 'On their hands they will bear you up, so that you will not dash your foot against a stone.'" Jesus answered him, "It is said, 'Do not put the Lord your God to the test.'" When the devil had finished every test, he departed from him until an opportune time.

(Luke 4:9–13)

Jesus's confrontation with the devil in the desert offered the early monks a valuable example in talking back to the devil's suggestions (see Matthew 4:1–11; Luke 4:1–13). In the initial temptation toward gluttony, Jesus was asked to change a stone into bread, thus suggesting a preoccupation with self-preservation. He instantly snapped back with a verse from the book of Deuteronomy. The second temptation concerned pride and self-gratification as the devil told Jesus he could presume angelic support in a precarious situation. Jesus retorted with another Scripture passage. Finally, the devil employed a temptation toward power and self-image, offering Jesus the kingdoms of the world if he would only worship him. Once again, Jesus talked back with a third verse, again from Deuteronomy.

The lesson offered to the desert monks and to us is obvious: don't fiddle and fuss with any tempting thought, trying to justify or rationalize what it might be asking of us; when we do, the slow dance of temptation begins as the devil wraps his claws around our minds and hearts and nudges us to commit the sins of pride, greed, anger, lust, gluttony, acedia, or envy. Instead, we cut off the temptation by confronting it head on, naming it for what it is, and retorting with the truth proclaimed in Scripture. Such an immediate response keeps us focused on our call to become little Christs.

Here's a random selection of Scripture quotes that the desert monks recommended and used in talking back to the devil's tempting thoughts:

Pride

Do not say to yourself, "My power and the might of my own hand have gotten me this wealth." But remember the Lord *your God, for it is he who gives you power to get wealth, so that he may confirm his covenant that he swore to your ancestors, as he is doing today.* (Deuteronomy 8:17–18)

Toward the scorners he is scornful, but to the humble he shows favor. (Proverbs 3:34)

Why do you see the speck in your neighbor's eye, but do not notice the log in your own eye? (Matthew 7:3)

For all who exalt themselves will be humbled, and those who humble themselves will be exalted. (Luke 14:11)

But by the grace of God I am what I am, and his grace toward me has not been in vain. On the contrary, I worked harder than any of them—though it was not I, but the grace of God that is within me. (1 Corinthians 15:10)

Greed

If any of your kin fall into difficulty and become dependent on you, you shall support them; they shall live with you as though resident aliens. (Leviticus 25:35)

Do not withhold good from those to whom it is due, when it is in your power to do it. Do not say to your neighbor, "Go, and come again, tomorrow I will give it"—when you have it with you. (Proverbs 3:27–28)

Do not store up for yourselves treasures on earth, where moth and rust consume and where thieves break in and steal. (Matthew 6:19)

Then Jesus looked around and said to his disciples, "How hard it will be for those who have wealth to enter the kingdom of God!" (Mark 10:23)

Keep your lives free from the love of money, and be content with what you have; for he has said, "I will never leave you or forsake you." (Hebrews 13:5)

Anger

Then he sent his brothers on their way, and as they were leaving he said to them, "Do not quarrel along the way." (Genesis 45:24)

Refrain from anger, and forsake wrath. Do not fret—it leads only to evil. (Psalm 37:8)

Whoever is slow to anger has great understanding, but one who has a hasty temper exalts folly. (Proverbs 14:29)

But I say to you that if you are angry with a brother or sister, you will be liable to judgment; and if you insult a brother or sister, you will be liable to the council; and if you say, "You fool," you will be liable to the hell of fire. (Matthew 5:22)

Be angry but do not sin; do not let the sun go down on your anger, and do not make room for the devil. (Ephesians 4:26–27)

Lust

You shall not covet your neighbor's house; you shall not covet your neighbor's wife, or male or female slave, or ox, or donkey, or anything that belongs to your neighbor. (Exodus 20:17)

Do not desire [another's wife's] beauty in your heart, and do not let her capture you with her eyelashes; for a prostitute's fee is only a loaf of bread, but the wife of another stalks a man's very life. (Proverbs 6:25–26)

But I say to you that everyone who looks at a woman with lust has already committed adultery with her in his heart. (Matthew 5:28)

Do not be deceived! Fornicators, idolaters, adulterers, male prostitutes, sodomites, thieves, the greedy, drunkards, revilers, robbers— none of these will inherit the kingdom of God. (1 Corinthians 6:9–10)

Be sure of this, that no fornicator or impure person, or one who is greedy (that is, an idolater), has any inheritance in the kingdom of Christ and of God. (Ephesians 5:5)

Gluttony

The LORD does not let the righteous go hungry, but he thwarts the craving of the wicked. (Proverbs 10:3)

Do not be among winebibbers, or among gluttonous eaters of meat; for the drunkard and the glutton will come to poverty, and drowsiness will clothe them with rags. (Proverbs 23:20–21)

Let us live honorably as in the day, not in reveling and drunkenness, not in debauchery and licentiousness, not in quarreling and jealousy. Instead, put on the Lord Jesus Christ, and make no provision for the flesh, to gratify its desires. (Romans 13:13–14)

Now, discipline always seems painful rather than pleasant at the time, but later it yields the peaceful fruit of righteousness to those who have been trained by it. (Hebrews 12:11)

Listlessness

Wait for the LORD, and keep to his way, and he will exalt you to inherit the land; you will look on the destruction of the wicked. (Psalm 37:34)

How long will you lie there, O lazybones? When will you rise from your sleep? A little sleep, a little slumber, a little folding of the hands to rest, and poverty will come upon you like a robber, and want, like an armed warrior. (Proverbs 6:9–11)

And everyone who has left houses or brothers or sisters or father or mother or children or fields, for my name's sake, will receive a hundredfold, and will inherit eternal life. (Matthew 19:29)

Rejoice in hope, be patient in suffering, persevere in prayer. (Romans 12:12)

For you need endurance, so that when you have done the will of God, you may receive what was promised. For yet "in a very little while, the one who is coming will come and will not delay; but my righteous one will live by faith. My soul takes no pleasure in anyone who shrinks back." (Hebrews 10:36–38)

Vainglory

Let another praise you, and not your own mouth—a stranger, and not your own lips. (Proverbs 27:2)

Beware of practicing your piety before others in order to be seen by them; for then you have no reward from your Father in heaven. (Matthew 6:1)

"Let the one who boasts, boast in the Lord." For it is not those who commend themselves that are approved, but those whom the Lord commends. (2 Corinthians 10:17–18)

Am I now seeking human approval, or God's approval? Or am I trying to please people? If I were still pleasing people, I would not be a servant of Christ. (Galatians 1:10)

Do not love the world or the things in the world. The love of the Father is not in those who love the world. (1 John 2:15)

Dejection

You are a hiding place for me; you preserve me from trouble; you surround me with glad cries of deliverance. (Psalm 32:7)

Do not rejoice over me, O my enemy; when I fall, I shall rise; when I sit in darkness, the LORD will be a light to me. (Micah 7:8)

Do not let your hearts be troubled. Believe in God, believe also in me. (John 14:1)

I consider that the sufferings of this present time are not worth comparing with the glory about to be revealed to us. (Romans 8:18)

For godly grief produces a repentance that leads to salvation and brings no regret, but worldly grief produces death. (2 Corinthians 7:10)

We are easily deceived and duped by temptation. That's why the desert Christians were quick to quote Jesus's hard teaching, "If your hand or your foot causes you to stumble, cut it off and throw it away; it is better for you to enter life maimed or lame than to have two hands or two feet and to be thrown into the eternal fire" (Matthew 18:8; see also Matthew 5:29–30; 18:9). We must remain single-hearted, not entertaining two masters (see Matthew 5:8; 6:24). "But strive first for the kingdom of God and his righteousness" (Matthew 6:33) is a clarion call to remain attentive and focused and to cut off any tempting thought as soon as it arises.

Other Strategies for Dealing with Temptations

How do we keep that attention and focus? By keeping vigilance over our thoughts and inner monologues. They are the devil's first line of seduction. As soon as we find ourselves justifying or rationalizing an action consistent with any of the eight tempting thoughts, we are not far from giving in to it. Simple awareness can be the beginning of cutting off temptation.

We also need to be vigilant over the heart's feelings and our cerebral reactions to situations. Feelings and emotions such as pride, lust, or anger are neither right nor wrong in themselves. They are neutral. They are typically the knee-jerk reactions of our heart. However, the way we entertain, express, or vent them will sometimes get us dancing with the devil and later committing sin.

We can so closely identify with a temptation that we begin to believe that we *are* the temptation and therefore cannot resist it. Our rationalization for giving in is simple: "This is just who I am." But in actuality we are all so much more than our superficial thoughts and the emotions they elicit from us.

Some temptations keep returning and discouraging or embarrassing us. The tempting thought of listlessness whispers, "Oh, you might as well give in, since you obviously haven't outgrown it." In this instance, it's important to remember that temptations will dissipate when we stand up and talk back to them. When they return, we talk back again. And again. And again. That's the very nature of temptations. They are desperate. They keep buzzing around until they find something on which to land.

I once co-preached a weekend retreat with Sean Herriott, host of *Morning Air* on the Relevant Radio Network. He offered us a keen insight: there is a dignity in doggedly standing up and stubbornly resisting temptation time and time again. That persistence speaks volumes about the fire in our lives and our commitment to the Spirit's transformative process.

Knowing ourselves and our weaknesses goes a long way in pinpointing where we need to be vigilant. Temptations rarely occur where we are strong and confident; if they do, we quickly talk back to them and cut them off. For example, I am usually fairly self-confident and feel secure about my life and the choices I have made. Consequently, I rarely am tempted toward envy; if I am, I quickly stand up to the tempting thought, and it immediately goes up in smoke. However, there are other areas in my life—in relationships and how I am so judgmental—where I am weak and stand on shaky ground. In these areas, I need to focus my attention, be vigilant, and pray for the strengthening grace of perseverance.

The desert fathers and mothers also remind us to be proactive in our struggles with temptations. Rather than simply waiting around until temptations arise and then talking back and resisting them, we are called to live the virtues that attack the very roots of the eight tempting thoughts. The proactive virtues (and the tempting thoughts they attack) are:

- charity (pride)
- generosity (greed)
- patience (anger)
- chastity (lust)
- self-control (gluttony)
- perseverance (listlessness)
- humility (vainglory)
- diligence (dejection)

These virtues aid the Spirit in transforming us into who we profess to be by virtue of our baptism: little Christs.

Blazing with the fire of godly enthusiasm is no easy task. It requires not only trust in the Spirit of God but also an awareness of and resistance to myriad temptations that come our way each and every day. We do not do that alone. Keep in mind that we also can rely upon the help of the great High Priest who was tempted in every way possible but never sinned (see Hebrews 4:15).

■ PRACTICE

Reflect upon a situation when your defenses are typically down. What tempting thought arises? Rehearse in your mind how you will talk back to the temptation with one of the recommended Scripture passages. Also commit to intentionally practicing the appropriate proactive virtue that challenges that tempting thought.

■ GO DEEPER

Louis J. Cameli, *The Devil You Don't Know: Recognizing and Resisting Evil in Everyday Life* (Notre Dame, IN: Ave Maria Press, 2011).

Evagrius of Pontus, *Talking Back. Antirrhetikos. A Monastic Handbook for Combating Demons*, translated with an introduction by David Brakke (Collegeville, MN: Cistercian Publications/Liturgical Press, 2009).

Mary Margaret Funk, *Thoughts Matter: The Practice of the Spiritual Life* (New York: Continuum, 1998).

CHAPTER 28

SURRENDER AND ABANDONMENT

■

As you are discovering, spiritual transformation and becoming all flame require more than God's grace, kindling, and spiritual practices that help fan the spark of God. They also require intentional commitments like the examination of conscience, forgiveness, and resisting temptations that are challenging and seemingly stretch us beyond our limits. And the commitments don't stop there.

Tony has multiple sclerosis and is in a wheelchair. I will never forget a conversation I had with him a few years ago.

"Father, I've been in this wheelchair now for more than fifteen years. I've begged God to heal me, to give me the grace to stand up, push this wheelchair away, and walk on my own. I've prayed and prayed and still get no reply. Why won't God answer my prayer?"

Using his right hand and hitting the right armrest of the wheelchair, he continued, his voice cracking with emotion, "This is the enemy. This is my chain of slavery."

"Tony," I said, tapping the right armrest, "this is not the enemy or a chain of slavery. This is your path to holiness. And the moment you can surrender and accept it is the moment you will be freed from it. Embrace it. Then you'll go on your way—*in* it."

The Cross in Our Lives

I know this lesson can be a difficult one to hear. We each have a cross that we have prayed to be delivered from or wish we could change. It could be a burden, worry, trial, tribulation, misfortune, hardship, misery, suffering, or sorrow; it might be cut and hewn in the form of a divorce, a friend's betrayal, the loss of a job, financial challenges, the diagnosis of a terminal illness, or the effects of a natural disaster. Whatever it is, we spend too much time and energy trying to walk away from it or refashion it in a way that is more acceptable to us.

Jesus himself experienced this human struggle as he faced his impending death. In the Garden of Gethsemane, he fell into a state of dreadful agony and prayed, "Father, if you are willing, remove this cup from me; yet, not my will but yours be done" (Luke 22:42). He struggled to live out his intention of abandonment. "In his anguish he prayed more earnestly, and his sweat became like great drops of blood falling down on the ground" (v. 44).

There is a clear emotional shift, however, evidenced in the way he peacefully submitted to being arrested (see verses 47–53), his refusal to offer a self-defense before the assembly of Jewish elders and Pilate (see vv. 66–71; 23:1–5), and his silence before Herod (see 23:9). Moreover, his final words from the cross boldly proclaim that his intention had become reality as he handed over his life to God: "Father, into your hands I commend my spirit" (23:46). In that final act of surrender and abandonment, Jesus lovingly offered one of his greatest gifts: faith and trust in God.

> If any want to become my followers, let them deny themselves and take up their cross and follow me.
>
> (Matthew 16:24)

Called to become little Christs, we must learn to accept the cross in our lives. Jesus makes this the prerequisite for every disciple. So important is this that the Gospel tradition repeats it five times (see Matthew 10:38; 16:24; Mark

8:34; Luke 9:23; 14:27). It provides indispensable kindling for the fire of godly enthusiasm.

The Act of Abandonment

I gradually became used to the Chinese culture and acclimatized to its living conditions. My previous struggles with adjustment had dissipated. I was confident with my language skills, had many local friends and a job as director of human resources for a large, international accounting firm that provided a resident/working visa to keep me legal while I ministered on weekends to Roman Catholics. I had settled in and just assumed I would spend the rest of my life as a "newfangled" missionary among the Chinese people.

One Sunday afternoon as I left my apartment to attend a meeting of parishioners, I noticed a marked "Security Police" automobile parked outside. The apartment's receptionist commented that two men had been inquiring about me, my activities, and my employment. As I got into a taxi to go to my meeting, the police started their car and followed me. It quickly became apparent that my cover had been blown and the Chinese government knew who I was, where I lived, and what I was doing. Realizing that my time as a Chinese missionary would have to come to an end, I got a lump in my throat.

Over the following weeks, I became depressed as I struggled to understand why God had brought me to the other side of the world only to have this happen after almost twelve years. During a phone conversation, a wise priest advised me, "Don't try and figure it out. Just accept it and trust that God has another adventure in store for you." It took me more than two months before I begrudgingly resigned myself to his advice.

Surrender and acceptance of the cross—be it a disappointment, misfortune, or sorrow—require an act of abandonment. One of the most difficult spiritual commitments, it demands that we put our faith and trust into action. It is a far cry from my own passive act of begrudging resignation, offered with a defenseless and defeated sigh, characterized by regret that smolders among the ashes.

The abandonment to God's will by Christian disciples is characterized by the trust known to mature believers. Think in terms of the fire of a lover's selflessness. Those who have been enflamed by that selflessness and trust willingly let go of the false self's wishes and its egotistical desires. They joyfully receive and respond to the needs or duties of the present moment, however taxing, painful, or inconvenient. They peacefully submit to whatever way the Spirit chooses to continue the transformative process of the spiritual life. This is the abandonment that shaped the life of Jesus—and should shape our lives as little Christs.

This abandonment requires what the spiritual tradition calls holy indifference. The English word *indifference* is unfortunate, because it implies living with careless apathy, irresponsible disinterest, or a hardened lack of concern. Holy indifference, however, means living from a place of interior freedom where one's heart is no longer constricted by egotistical demands but burns with a faith crackling with trust in God.

Floating in water provides a useful analogy. The more we struggle to float in a swimming pool—and consequently maintain control—the more we will fail and sink to the bottom. Floating requires that we let go and give ourselves over to the water. It requires a kind of trust in the buoyancy of water.

The same is true with the abandonment born of holy indifference; it requires trust and is not about resignation. As when we let go and give ourselves over to the water, we surrender ourselves and willingly submit to the mystery of life that God sets before us. That includes actively yielding to things we are powerless to change, knowing that God is ever-present and trusting that the Spirit is at work. We deliberately pick up that cross. We embrace it. And in our acceptance, surrender, and embrace, the God who yearns to be in a relationship with us transforms us into people of godly enthusiasm who will know the power of the Resurrection.

Charles de Foucauld, beatified by the Catholic Church in 2005, surrendered to the cross as a martyr in Algeria, North Africa, in 1916. He wrote a prayer that captures the spirit of abandonment that Jesus himself had and that we are all called to have as little Christs. This is the prayer offered by the surrendered, accepting heart:

> Father,
> I abandon myself into your hands.
> Do with me what you will.
> Whatever you may do, I thank you.
> I am ready for all, I accept all.
> Let only your will be done in me
> and in all your creatures.
> I wish no more than this, O Lord.
> Into your hands I commend my soul.
> I offer it to you with all the love of my heart,
> for I love you, Lord, and so need to give myself,
> to surrender myself into your hands

without reserve and with boundless confidence,
for you are my Father.[18]

■ PRACTICE

Commit to slowly and meditatively praying Charles de Foucauld's prayer of abandonment for an entire week—then memorizing it. When you find yourself fighting against the cross in your life, pray it as a way to strengthen your own surrender and abandonment.

■ GO DEEPER

David G. Benner, *Surrender to Love: Discovering the Heart of Christian Spirituality* (Downers Grove, IL: InterVarsity Press, 2003).

Albert Haase, OFM, "The Practice of Surrender," http://www.youtube.com/watch?v=Fg5Xk2ejlOQ.

Albert Haase, OFM, *This Sacred Moment: Becoming Holy Right Where You Are* (Downers Grove, IL: InterVarsity Press, 2010).

Jean Pierre de Caussade, *The Joy of Full Surrender* (Brewster, MA: Paraclete Press, 2008).

CHAPTER 29

REVEAL EVERYTHING TO GOD

∎

Spiritual transformation is about growing in intimacy with God. And intimacy requires vulnerability and openness—the kind of vulnerability and openness you show when you reveal *everything* to your beloved. This is a commitment to total and complete honesty.

Many Christians find that keeping a spiritual journal helps to foster that commitment. Unlike a regular journal that typically records the *facts* of our lives (who, what, when, where, why), a spiritual journal records our *feelings* (joy, sadness, fear, disappointment, peacefulness, anger, discouragement, frustration, etc.), *impressions* ("this could possibly mean that . . ."), *hunches* ("my gut tells me . . ."), and *responses* ("my immediate reaction was . . .") to the facts of our lives, especially in regard to the process of being transformed by the Spirit of God. In a spiritual journal, we have a heart-to-heart conversation, conveying the contours of the soul in script.

As you sit down to write in your spiritual journal, consciously choose not to be distracted by the cellphone, the doorbell, or the timer on the oven. This is sacred time that deserves your respect and reverence. As in or with other moments and movements of grace, give yourself over to the process; surrender to any amount of time the process might ask of you. You don't want to be rushed as you reflect and write.

Start in silence. Closing your eyes, breathing deeply, and sipping some coffee or tea are great ways to settle down and become attentive as you ponder and pray over your life. You might want to say a prayer to the Holy Spirit before starting to explore this moment or event in the history of your own transformation.

It's best to date each entry. This can be helpful in the future when you want to retrieve your feelings and reactions to different experiences. It also provides a historical context for your spiritual growth and awareness.

Write honestly and naturally—whether that be quickly or deliberately, not allowing the inner critic to edit or delete anything considered inappropriate. You don't have to write eloquently or even in complete sentences; after all, you're writing for yourself and not for an audience. This openness, vulnerability, and honesty breed divine revelation and self-revelation; they are the building blocks of intimacy.

> Your very lives are a letter that anyone can read by just looking at you. Christ himself wrote it—not with ink, but with God's living Spirit; not chiseled into stone, but carved into human lives—and we publish it.
>
> (2 Corinthians 3:3, THE MESSAGE)

When journaling, I begin by answering the questions used in preparation for a spiritual direction appointment:

- What is the most important thing going on in my life right now, and how do I feel about it?
- What is God doing in my life right now?
- Where and how is the Spirit nudging me?
- How am I responding to God's call in my daily life?
- What am I deliberately fighting against or resisting?

Your journal doesn't have to consist only of sentences. As they say, a picture is worth a thousand words. Sometimes a doodle, photograph, or newspaper advertisement says it best! Or a metaphor or simile might spontaneously come to mind that captures exactly where you are: "I feel as if the sun is setting, and I am sinking in quicksand." Perhaps we have seen something in nature that triggers a memory, a feeling, or an insight: "I saw that bird feed her chicks and instantly thought how God has been nursing me in the past few weeks."

When I first started journaling, I used to get discouraged, thinking I had to write in my journal every day. Nothing could be further from the truth. Some seasons in life call me to write daily; others call me to write weekly or monthly. It's important to discover personally the frequency and rhythm that work best.

Each of the four annual seasons provides an opportune time for Bradley, one of my spiritual directees, to review his past journal entries. Sometimes, in looking over what he has written over a particular season, he discovers in hindsight an important thread of God's grace weaving together the story of his life. Sometimes it is in reading past entries that he experiences God's revelation—"Oh, now I get it," he says to himself—or comes to a deeper awareness of himself and how he is responding to the action of God's Spirit. Some people follow Bradley's practice of reading past entries when an opportunity arises. Other people, like Sherry, don't find it helpful to read past entries; for them, the instant revelation that sometimes comes during the process of writing is helpful enough. You'll soon discover what's useful for you.

Other Journal Entries

A spiritual journal can also include "ah-ha" moments of divine revelation: new insights into Scripture, biblical prayers that we find meaningful, and passages from spiritual books that are worth highlighting and remembering. It can also document our sins, hurts, limitations, longings, discernment processes, insights, and deepest desires.

In the back of my own spiritual journal, as I read past entries, I keep a running list titled "What Life Has Taught Me about God and Myself." I record the date and state the insight or realization, followed in parentheses by the event in my life to which it refers. Here's an example:

September 17, 1980. God is my father who will never abandon me (Dad's suicide and the financial consequences that followed it in 1968).

Here's another example:

November 8, 2011. Gratitude keeps me aware that my talents are gifts freely given by God. Talents are not my property, and I am not a "self-made" man (the invitation from a publisher to write a book for them).

This ongoing list becomes a document of God's revelation and my own self-awareness.

A spiritual journal can also be "a sanctuary in script" where we go for intimate conversations with God and others. We might write a letter to God—or have God write a letter to us. We might write out a dialogue with a deceased relative, a person from Scripture, or even an individual from the history of Christian spirituality who has influenced us. Though this kind of writing might feel awkward or contrived at first, giving ourselves over to the process can provide the grace for gaining a deeper understanding of others, for healing old emotional wounds, and for providing closure to unresolved issues in past relationships.

The spiritual journal is meant to increase our sensitivity to the Spirit's transformative process and our commitment to being vulnerable, open, and honest with God. Any writing technique that helps to foster that sensitivity and intimacy is well worth trying. For many of us, the journal becomes our go-to place for pondering and treasuring the gifts, graces, and blessings bestowed upon the heart.

▪ PRACTICE

Commit a few hours to reflecting upon your entire life: your earliest memories, your childhood, your adolescence, and the choices and decisions you have made in adulthood. Take your time with this process. Then begin to write out your own list entitled, "What Life Has Taught Me about God and Myself." What do these statements tell you about God's enthusiasm to be in a relationship with you, and about your response?

▪ GO DEEPER

Christina Baldwin, *Life's Companion: Journal Writing as a Spiritual Quest* (New York: Bantam, 1990).

Helen Cepero, *Journaling as a Spiritual Practice: Encountering God through Attentive Writing* (Downers Grove, IL: InterVarsity Press, 2008).

Francis Dorff, O. PRAEM., *Simply SoulStirring: Writing as a Meditative Practice* (Mahwah, NJ: Paulist Press, 1998).

Ron Klug, *How to Keep a Spiritual Journal: A Guide to Journal Keeping for Inner Growth and Personal Discovery*, Revised Edition (Minneapolis: Augsburg, 2002).

CHAPTER 30

SILENCE AND SOLITUDE: THE RETREAT

■

The intimacy required in becoming a little Christ takes more than the vulnerability, openness, and honesty we bring to keeping a spiritual journal. It also requires a commitment to spending time with a God whom "no one has ever seen" (see 1 John 4:12). Though there are many ways to do that—in prayer or loving service, for example—one of the most challenging ways is in the silence and solitude of a retreat.

I know people who feel threatened by the hush of silence and the loneliness of solitude. They maneuver themselves into real or virtual relationships and conversations or turn on the television or find some other way to run from the dreaded S&S. But authentic spiritual transformation does not allow us to escape the need for silence and solitude.

Silence compels us to unplug the noise in our lives, to close our mouths, and to confront the vast, arid expanse within us. The psalmist enjoins us, "Be still and know that I am God! I am exalted among the nations, I am exalted in the earth" (Psalm 46:10), or, as Eugene Peterson graphically paraphrases it, "Step out of the traffic! Take a long, loving look at me, your High God, above politics, above everything" (THE MESSAGE). Unfortunately, most of us prefer the racket of the traffic to the stillness of silence.

Solitude challenges us to break away from family and friends and come to grips with the junk food stuffed in our lunch boxes and the clutter hoarded and stacked against the walls in our hearts. It is the place where, according to Henri Nouwen, we remove the "scaffolding"[19] of our lives: friends, telephone calls, meetings, music, and books. It's where, without all our props and diplomas, we stand naked before the living God and confront the reality of who we *really* are and not who we dress to be every day. "What you are before God, that you are and nothing more."[20] Far from a spiritual spa or therapeutic clinic, solitude is, as Nouwen rightly notes, "the furnace of transformation."[21]

The Desert of the Annual Retreat

Jesus, full of the Holy Spirit, returned from the Jordan and was led by the Spirit in the wilderness, where for forty days he was tempted by the devil. He ate nothing at all during those days, and when they were over, he was famished. . . . But now more than ever the word about Jesus spread abroad; many crowds would gather to hear him and to be cured of their diseases. But he would withdraw to deserted places and pray.

(Luke 4:1–2; 5:15–16)

According to the Gospels, immediately after Jesus's baptism, the Spirit led him into the solitude of the desert (see Matthew 4:1–11; Mark 1:12–13; Luke 4:1–13). This was like a training camp at which Jesus confronted his enemy. The circumstance and the weeks of prayer no doubt confirmed in him the purpose of his mission and the passion for his Father's will. He emerged from the desert "proclaiming the good news of God and saying, 'The time is fulfilled, and the kingdom of God has come near; repent, and believe in the good news'" (Mark 1:14–15). After his desert time, Jesus was "filled with the power of the Spirit" (Luke 4:14) and would periodically retreat again into silence and solitude (see Luke 5:16; Mark 1:35).

Like many other people, I find an annual retreat to be an important time to intentionally follow Jesus into silence and solitude. In many respects, it is a deliberate extension of my daily prayer time. Leaving my cellphone and computer behind, I temporarily retreat from my present surroundings, disengage from my relationships, and confront the noise and trinkets in my life. This helps to reignite my passion and enthusiasm as I surrender to the Spirit's process of transforming me into a little Christ.

Kinds of Retreats

Over the past thirty-five years, I have discovered that a retreat can take on a variety of forms.

The *thirty-day Ignatian retreat* (often called the Spiritual Exercises) is done once, at most twice, in life and was designed by St. Ignatius of Loyola not only to help participants discover God's presence in their lives but also to help foster a personal commitment to becoming little Christs. The person making the retreat goes to a retreat house for thirty consecutive days of prayer and reflection. The person spends four to six hours a day meditating upon selected Scriptures based on four successive themes and then meets every day with a director to share the fruits of the meditations.

For those like me unable to take off thirty consecutive days for solitude, Ignatius designed the *retreat in daily life* (called the Nineteenth Annotation). Offering the basic dynamic of the thirty-day retreat, it can take place at home during the course of daily routines and job responsibilities. Conducted over a period of several months to more than a year, it requires daily prayer and scriptural meditation. A retreatant typically meets once a week or every two weeks with a director to discuss his or her reflections on the Scriptures. This format offered me the opportunity to try out in real life what I was learning and discovering in the course of the retreat. Creighton University offers a popular online version.

Preached weekend retreats usually begin on Thursday or Friday evening and last until Sunday noon. In an atmosphere of silence and solitude at a retreat house, a preacher will be invited to offer four to six thirty-minute talks on a specific theme, such as the Beatitudes, the Lord's Prayer, women in Scripture, the gifts of the Holy Spirit, or some other topic chosen by the preacher. Between these large-group sessions, retreatants spend time walking, meditating, journaling, reading, praying the Stations of the Cross, and perhaps celebrating the Sacrament of Reconciliation. Preached retreats are offered in most Catholic retreat houses across the United States.

Similar to preached retreats, *guided retreats* feature a preacher. In a guided retreat, there is usually only one extended conference or talk per day, lasting forty-five minutes to an hour. Afterward, those making the retreat spend the rest of the day in silence and solitude reflecting upon what they have heard. In the evening, there might be an optional group sharing or prayer service, based upon the theme of the day's conference.

Directed retreats are tailor-made, focused on an individual's specific needs. They can last anywhere from a weekend to a week. I make a weeklong directed retreat every two years and appreciate meeting with an assigned director every day during the retreat for twenty to thirty minutes. I discuss with the director some issue in my life that I am struggling with or discerning, or how I am or am not responding to the transformative grace of the Holy Spirit in my life. On occasion, the director has given me homework to do for the day, such as reading and meditating upon a passage of Scripture. I think the advantage of a directed retreat is that it allows for as much or as little wiggle room as a person is looking for. Think of it as an intensive period of spiritual direction with an assigned director who listens to you with a pair of ears different from your usual spiritual director and offers his or her own thoughts, comments, and insights.

The years I don't make a directed retreat, I make a *private retreat.* This is a self-designed retreat. I go to a retreat house or hermitage to be alone. I'm on my own as I plan my daily schedule, sometimes my meals, and how I will spend my time. Everyone does private retreats differently, but I typically spend part of every day in extended prayer, reading a book or praying with Scripture, reflecting upon the past year, and journaling. I also take a long walk. Of all the different kinds of retreats, the private retreat was the most intimidating for me initially, since it comes the closest to providing the experience of the silence and solitude of Jesus in the desert.

No matter how they are packaged, the silence and solitude experienced in a retreat are important. By stripping us of our iPods and tablets, and the distractions of other creature comforts, a retreat challenges us to recommit again to stoking the flame of godly enthusiasm in our lives.

■ PRACTICE

Go online to find a nearby retreat center. If you have trouble finding one, contact your local church for suggestions and recommendations. Get information about the retreat center's upcoming retreats and commit to making one within the next year. If you've never made a retreat before, it's wise not to bite off more than you can chew;

choose a preached weekend retreat and start there. While on retreat, write about the experience in a journal. After the retreat, discuss your experience with your spiritual director.

■ GO DEEPER

An Online Retreat: A 34 Week Retreat for Everyday Life, http://onlineministries.creighton.edu/CollaborativeMinistry/cmo-retreat.html.

Gus Gordon, *Solitude and Compassion: The Path to the Heart of the Gospel* (Maryknoll, NY: Orbis, 2009).

Thomas M. Santa, *Sacred Refuge: Why and How to Make a Retreat* (Notre Dame, IN: Ave Maria Press, 2005).

Robert Sardello, *Silence: The Mystery of Wholeness* (Berkeley: North Atlantic Books, 2008).

CHAPTER 31

SABBATH REST

■

The transformation into a Christlike flame blazing in the world isn't accomplished simply by *doing* things in response to God's grace. Paradoxically, it also requires a dynamic commitment that gives us cause to pause—literally! Becoming all flame is as much about *being* as it is about *doing*.

A friend told me his life was "like being driven in an old, clunky automobile with a stuck gas pedal; it's going to stop by either running into something or running out of gas." That description fits so many of us: we are driven workaholics whose lives are potentially out of control and headed in a fatal direction.

In our work-obsessed world, the spiritual practice of taking a day off is countercultural. The Sabbath rest appears downright unnatural. The very word *Sabbath*, derived from the Hebrew for "stop, cease, desist, pause, rest," indicates that such rest requires a deliberate act of the will. For some of us, that will sound like fingernails scratching against the blackboard.

Scriptural Foundations

The religious origins of the weekly Sabbath, from Friday sundown to Saturday sundown, are rooted in the Jewish Scriptures. While wandering in the desert, the Israelites were told that the seventh day of the week was "a day of solemn rest, a holy sabbath to the LORD" (Exodus 16:23) when all work was forbidden (see

Exodus 20:8–10; 31:13–17; Deuteronomy 5:12–14). Though the prohibitions against various kinds of work, such as lighting fires, cooking, and pressing grapes (see Exodus 16:23, 35:3; Nehemiah 13:15) strike twenty-first-century ears as overly detailed and maybe even picayune, the explicit point was that this day was meant to be a break in the action, an armistice from the daily grind and drudgery, a day of joyful and peaceful relaxation.

The Sabbath was sacred because it was a sign of the covenant made with Moses and his descendants on Mt. Sinai (see Exodus 31:13). It acknowledged God as the Creator of time and the universe and allowed the Israelites to experience the rest that God himself had experienced (Exodus 31:17; see also 20:11). It also reminded the chosen people of their former slavery in Egypt and the wonderful Exodus wrought by God on their behalf (Deuteronomy 5:15). And so the Sabbath was a weekly reminder to the Israelites of who God is and what God did to satisfy his fiery passion to be in a relationship with them.

The Sabbath was made for humankind, and not humankind for the Sabbath.

(Mark 2:27)

By the time of Jesus, the Sabbath rest as interpreted by the scribes and Pharisees had become a legalistic yoke and burden. With stunning insight, Jesus retrieved its original intention. It once again became a restful and leisurely celebration of God's enthusiasm for the chosen people.

Though a former strict observer of the Jewish law, Paul did not consider the Sabbath as obligatory for Christians (see Colossians 2:16; Galatians 4:9–10;

Romans 14:5), especially as Christianity attracted more and more Gentiles and the Jewish Christian churches disappeared. Sunday quickly replaced Saturday and became the Lord's Day, when Christians gathered and broke bread together in the Eucharist (see Acts 20:7; 1 Corinthians 16:2). The first day of the week was chosen, it being the day of Christ's resurrection; it represented new life and a new creation.

Rest as Sacred Time

In our compulsive, work-driven culture, observing Sabbath rest is perceived to be wasting time that could be better served in productivity. So why do we get off the driven treadmill of routine? Because there is something holy and Godlike about deliberately choosing to give ourselves a break and entering into the Creator's experience of resting and being refreshed. A famous shoe commercial used to push us to lace up our shoes and "Just do it." Similarly, the practice of Sabbath rest challenges us to remove our shoes as Moses did before the burning bush, prop up our feet, and just be. Like God on the seventh day of creation, we look back on the fruits of our week's labors and we enjoy them. We gather up the loose and frazzled corners of our lives and for this sacred time bring them together as a way of honoring who we are before God. Sabbath rest is about refreshment, reflection, and recollection. As the Jewish theologian Abraham Joshua Heschel insightfully writes in *The Sabbath: Its Meaning for Modern Man*, "It must always be remembered that the Sabbath is not an occasion for diversion or frivolity; not a day to shoot fireworks or to turn somersaults, but an opportunity to mend our tattered lives; to collect rather than to dissipate time."[22]

There are myriad ways to take advantage of this "opportunity," as Heschel calls it. They include the following:

- Celebrate the Eucharist in your parish and offer the fruits of your week's labors along with the bread and wine.
- Take a walk in the park or in a nearby arboretum and experience the fruits of God's labors found in creation.
- Spend some quality time with a spouse or a good friend.
- Read a biography, novel, or magazine (something other than what you read for work); take a nap or watch some television.
- Do something creative like painting, writing a poem, gardening, practicing a musical instrument, or knitting a sweater.
- Visit a zoo.
- Do the crossword puzzle in the newspaper or a Sudoku puzzle—or a jigsaw puzzle.
- Make a list of the "Top Ten Things I'm Grateful For."
- Plan a meal you've always wanted to try—and then cook it.
- Go out jogging or shoot a few hoops of basketball.
- Catch up with a friend or relative on the telephone.
- Take a neighbor, nephew, or niece out to the movies or invite them over to watch a DVD.
- Spend time in prayer or spiritual reading.

We enter into the authentic spirit of Sabbath rest when we choose a project or task that we enjoy *doing*; that makes it different from a project that we enjoy getting done. Without always being aware of the benefits, our lives get mended and time gets "collected" in the process of the doing. We begin to feel whole again; we catch our breath and anticipate the coming week. This spiritual practice was custom-made for humankind and is about a life-giving form of recreation as we celebrate Christ's re-creation at Easter.

Though the spiritual practice of Sabbath rest traditionally refers to an entire day, it can also be celebrated in short blocks of time during the week when we find ourselves running out of gas or spinning out of control. The stereotypical boss or inner voice might bark, "Don't just stand there—*do something*!" And yet the spiritual tradition of Sabbath rest responds, "Don't just do something—*stand there*." Take a break. Stop and relax. Taking such Sabbath time becomes another way of stoking the fire of godly enthusiasm as we respond to Jesus's invitation to turn off at a rest stop: "Come away to a deserted place all by yourselves and rest a while" (Mark 6:31). In those moments, we discover the rest and refreshment that only the Lord can give (see Matthew 11:28–30).

■ PRACTICE

Spend a large portion of a day, or even an entire day if your circumstances permit, doing nothing but relaxing and resting. Just lollygag and dawdle. Unless you like to cook, consider treating yourself to a meal out. If finances permit, invite a friend and go to a day spa. Don't journal about this. Don't reflect upon it. Just enjoy!

■ GO DEEPER

Lynne M. Baab, *Sabbath Keeping: Finding Freedom in the Rhythms of Rest* (Downers Grove, IL: IVP Books, 2005).

Marva Dawn, *Keeping the Sabbath Wholly: Ceasing, Resting, Embracing, Feasting* (Grand Rapids, MI: Eerdmans, 1989).

Martha Whitmore Hickman, *A Day of Rest: Creating a Spiritual Space in Your Week* (New York: Avon Books, 1999).

CHAPTER 32

PILGRIMAGE

■

I knelt in prayer in the small church of San Damiano, located outside the city walls of Assisi, Italy. It was where Francis of Assisi, early on in the process of his spiritual transformation, prayed for guidance, direction, and insight. The earliest biographies state he heard a voice from the crucifix saying, "Francis, rebuild my church, which as you see is falling into ruin." That was the spark that set him ablaze and transformed him into a beacon of light for a smoldering medieval Church.

I had come from the suburbs of Chicago to this little Italian church on pilgrimage. Like Francis, I too was looking for guidance, direction, and insight, and I could think of no better place to seek them than in this little church that was so influential in Francis's life. I was completing my doctoral studies and was discerning my ministry: a professor in the classroom or a preacher on the road?

I spent the afternoon in that church. I prayed, reflected, read the story of Jesus calling his disciples in the fifth chapter of Luke's Gospel, and journaled. I didn't hear any heavenly voice as Francis had. But my pilgrimage to San Damiano did give me an insight that illumined my discernment process and has shaped me for the past twenty-five years: God speaks in the events of my life; it is important that I be attentive and reflect upon them—now, more than ever.

An Ancient Practice

Perhaps it is asking a lot for you to consider committing to pilgrimage as an important step on your journey of transformation. But I am nevertheless asking you to consider it—for centuries of reasons.

Going on pilgrimage is a spiritual practice that dates back to the ancient church. For the better part of two millennia, Christian pilgrims have traveled to the land of Jesus's life and death not only to encounter the sacred places of our faith but also to be challenged by Jesus's call to become little Christs. The spiritual practice of pilgrimage soon expanded to praying at the tombs of Peter and Paul in Rome, walking the *camino* (road) to the tomb of the apostle James in Santiago de Compostela in Spain, and visiting places made special by the lives of Francis of Assisi (Italy), Ignatius of Loyola (Spain), Juan Diego (Mexico), Bernadette Soubirous (France), Junipero Serra (United States), André Bessette (Canada), and hundreds of other saintly men and women.

Just because we travel to another place doesn't mean we are going on pilgrimage. Indeed, there are a number of significant differences between tourists and pilgrims. Tourists depart with passports, digital cameras, laptops, and credit cards in hand. Prepared against any inconvenience and hoping to avoid any hassle, tourists travel accompanied by family and sometimes friends with the express purpose of seeing Arizona's Grand Canyon, London's Buckingham Palace, or Rome's Coliseum. Their trip is enhanced with leisurely visits to galleries, museums, cafés, and souvenir shops. In short, it's a vacation.

Pilgrims, on the other hand, though they might look like tourists on the surface, are really explorers. Their journey to a different place is really an interior journey to a deeper place. They leave the familiar exterior surroundings of their home to go to often-unfamiliar surroundings within. This interior journey might prove to be like the physical journey with its own inconvenience, loss of control, and adaptation to new customs and languages. For some who just recently began to catch the fire of godly enthusiasm, the unfamiliar landscapes of their own souls might mirror the sometimes exotic scenes outside.

Pilgrims bring their Bibles and journals; they don't primarily travel to sightsee but to "soulsee"—to self-explore, to reflect, and to open themselves more deeply to the transforming process of the Spirit. That was the purpose of my pilgrimage to San Damiano. I could have easily gone soulseeing at home—I often do so!—but some locations are thin places that have the power to open us to God's grace in unique and unforeseeable ways.

Pilgrims often travel with other pilgrims, with whom they gradually form a community that reflects the pilgrim church on earth. As such, they spend time praying both alone and communally. Rather than being encouraged to invest in souvenirs, pilgrims are challenged to divest themselves so that they can be molded in a truer way into little Christs. Their departure and journey to a sacred site, filled with self-reflection, prayer, and sometimes inconveniences and hassles, are *just as important* as their arrival.

The Practice of Pilgrimage

Unlike the motivation to visit an all-inclusive resort in Bali or an ancient monument like Stonehenge—relaxation, curiosity, adventure—the practice of pilgrimage begins with a spiritual desire, a call. I felt drawn to the little church of San Damiano because of its sacred significance in my Franciscan tradition and its potential for stoking the fire of godly enthusiasm in my life. Other pilgrims want to pray on the Mount of the Beatitudes; in the Garden of Gethsemane; on LaVerna, where Saint Francis received the stigmata; or at the grotto where the Blessed Mother appeared at Lourdes. We feel called to go to sacred sites to pray for others, to give thanks, to fulfill a promise, to ask for forgiveness, or to pray for a miracle.

Preparation. Pilgrimage begins with prayer and penance. To be led to a spiritual place within, we spend time in reflection, getting in touch with our spiritual desire to travel to a sacred place. If you are going to the Holy Land, you might want to read through one of the Gospels as a way to refresh your memory about the significance of various places in Jesus's life. If you are visiting a shrine made popular by a saint's life, it's wise to read about the saintly virtue of the person ahead of time. In preparation for my pilgrimage to Assisi, I read the earliest account of the life of Saint Francis, written two years after his death.

A day or two before leaving, Catholic pilgrims might want to attend Mass and celebrate the Sacrament of Reconciliation as a way to prepare for the upcoming spiritual journey.

Carry no purse, no bag, no sandals. . . . Whatever house you enter, first say, "Peace to this house!". . . Remain in the same house, eating and drinking whatever they provide.

(Luke 10:4, 5, 7)

The way of the pilgrim. We do not set out on our spiritual journey anticipating sumptuous food, comfortable transportation, and five-star hotels. We travel instead with the missionary spirit suggested by Jesus: detached, unencumbered, willing to accept any accommodation and whatever food is set before us (see Luke 9:1–5; 10:8). Pilgrimage also requires a lot of physical walking, which can be both challenging and exhausting. We presume that glitches and difficulties will occur; when they do, we notice our immediate reactions. The pilgrim's way challenges us to be patient, gentle with ourselves, and ever attentive and aware of the interior depths we are discovering while on the exterior journey to our pilgrim site. What happens *as* we travel *is* pilgrimage and forms an important part of this spiritual practice.

Along with patient, gentle self-awareness, we are called to foster three other attitudes. The first is to let go of any expectations. Those who deliberately seek out spiritual experiences and emotional highs will inevitably be disappointed; the God who journeyed with the Israelites in the desert and took on flesh in the forgotten town of Bethlehem has proven to be a God of surprise and disguise. While on the train from Rome to Assisi, I told myself not to expect the San Damiano crucifix to speak to me as it had to Francis; I knew that expectations turn a pilgrimage into an expedition and cause us to miss the grace that often catches us off-guard in the present moment.

Another pilgrim attitude is the willingness to receive and offer acts of charity. As pilgrims, we are humble enough to receive hospitality from locals and allow them to attend to our needs. We are also generous enough to aid those in our group needing help as well as to offer alms to the poor and needy we encounter on the way. This willingness strengthens the awareness of our interdependence and the fact that together we make up the body of Christ.

While on the way, we make a concerted effort to find time for solitude, prayer, and reflection. Making a pilgrimage is essentially an interior journey that reveals the geography of the soul. We need time to ponder this terrain and discover its burning bushes. Without prayer and reflection, the pilgrimage loses its potential and power as a transforming process of the Spirit.

Arrival. If we have been faithful to self-awareness, having few expectations and having humility, generosity, and prayer while on pilgrimage, our arrival at the sacred site will be symbolic of a new interior place in which we find ourselves. And with the new interior place comes a new potential for transformation.

While at the sacred site, we pray with any Scripture passage associated with the setting. Through imaginative prayer, we can place ourselves at the commemorated event. Afterward, to preserve the memory of the experience, we can journal about the emotions that arose, what we discovered about God and ourselves, and what spiritual challenge or gift this site offered to us.

Praying at the tomb of holy men and women, we ask the Holy Spirit to transform us into little Christs sent to respond lovingly to the unmet need or required duty of the present moment. We ask the saints to intercede and help us surrender, as they did, to the Spirit's promptings and process.

Returning Home. We keep the memory of the pilgrimage alive by listening closely to Gospel readings at Mass. A site is mentioned and we can say, "I was there!" We can also honor again the particular saint of the day. It's helpful to occasionally reread pilgrimage journals. Such practices keep us mindful that the God who has a burning desire to be in a relationship with us has himself come down on pilgrimage in the sacrament of the present moment.

And when we find ourselves physically incapable or financially unable to make another pilgrimage to a specific destination, we can rediscover the purpose of pilgrimage right where we are by walking again the interior highway of the heart to Mt. Zion in prayer (see Psalm 84:5).

■ PRACTICE

Spend time reflecting upon the sacred sites and places of pilgrimage that you feel drawn to. If one of them is local, consider an afternoon pilgrimage to it. If they are associated with Jesus or the early disciples in the Middle East, spend time with the appropriate Scripture passage; if with a saint, read about the person. If finances permit, commit to getting information and making a pilgrimage. If finances do not permit, visit a local bookstore or travel store and buy a pictorial guide to the place. Engage the location with the imaginative prayer technique mentioned in chapter 15 or use a version of lectio divina mentioned in chapter 14 with a work of its art.

■ GO DEEPER

Jim Forest, *Road to Emmaus: Pilgrimage as a Way of Life* (Maryknoll, NY: Orbis Books, 2007).

Christian George, *Sacred Travels: Recovering the Ancient Practice of Pilgrimage* (Downers Grove, IL: IVP Books, 2006).

Phileena Heuertz, *Pilgrimage of a Soul: Contemplative Spirituality for the Active Life* (Downers Grove, IL: IVP Books, 2010).

Edward Cletus Sellner, *Pilgrimage (Exploring a Great Spiritual Practice)* (Notre Dame, IN: Sorin Books, 2004).

CHAPTER 33

SOUL TRAINING

■

Fire and the heat that radiates from it cleanse and sterilize imperfections and impurities from an object as it is being transformed. The same is true for us as we become more and more Christlike by the power of the Holy Spirit. That's why there's one final commitment you need to consider, and it's the most challenging of all.

Stephen, a spiritual directee of mine, once asked, "What's the purpose of doing penance and acts of asceticism? Sometimes I do them to express sorrow for my sins; but then there are other times when I think of them as a kind of spiritual workout or soul training. Which is correct?"

Stephen's question gave me cause to pause and reconsider the motivation and intention behind all spiritual practices.

The Purpose of Practice

There is a wide range of spiritual practices: different methods of prayer, the examination of conscience, journaling, and pilgrimage, to name just a few of the ones we've explored in these pages. These practices do not make God present, for God pervades our very existence like the air we breathe: "In [God] we live and move and have our being" (Acts 17:28). Instead, they help to deepen our awareness of God and foster sensitivity to the "fullness of him who fills all in all" (Ephesians 1:23): the divine presence within us as well as the divine presence we encounter in the sacraments, in Scripture, in creation, in the events of our lives, and in our neighbor. In effect, they stoke the fire of godly enthusiasm and help to keep it burning in our lives.

Acts of penance and asceticism have their own traditional place within the range of spiritual practices. Acts of penance are often done in response to the awareness of our sinfulness before the presence of God. Acts of asceticism are also forms of "soul training," to use Stephen's expression; that is, we practice them to strengthen ourselves against the false self and its obsession with self-concern, self-image, self-gratification, and self-preservation. The three great practices of penance and asceticism taught by Jesus are prayer, fasting, and almsgiving.

In the Gospel of Matthew, Jesus places these three practices at the very center of the Sermon on the Mount. We are to give alms in secret so that we do not receive the praise of others (see 6:2–4). Prayer should be direct, succinct, and done behind closed doors (see 6:5–8). Fasting, like almsgiving and prayer, should not call attention to itself or be noticed by others (see 6:16–18). Though Jesus tells us *how* they should be practiced—in secret, not calling attention to themselves—he remains silent on *why* they should be practiced.

But Jesus's Jewish tradition would have provided the reasons for prayer, fasting, and almsgiving. The Hebrew Scriptures are filled with references to the prayers of thanksgiving, confession, petition, and intercession (see, e.g., 2 Kings 6:17; Psalm 95:2; Daniel 9:3–21; Sirach 51:13); the multitude of references all suggest prayer as our method of communicating with God. Fasting is a way to express contrition and a sincere intent to change one's ways (see, e.g., 1 Samuel 7:6; Jonah 3:5); Isaiah broadened its understanding to express a desire to turn away from injustice against, oppression of, and insensitivity toward the poor and needy (see, e.g., Isaiah 58:6–7). Almsgiving makes us aware of the interdependence between us and the poor, the aliens, the widows, and orphans (see Exodus 23:11; Deuteronomy 14:29).

Restoring Harmony

I value and respect the time-honored Jewish rationale for the three traditional practices of penance and asceticism—communication with God, conversion, and awareness of our interdependence. But I think there's another reason we should intentionally commit to these practices.

The Garden of Eden is the biblical symbol for the way God created this world and intended it to be. All of creation was intricately connected and interdependent. Adam and Eve felt no shame before each other and naturally experienced the presence of God in the "evening breeze" (Genesis 3:8). In this paradise, there was harmony and balance among God, self, and others.

But at some point, the false self with its obsessive self-centered desires made its appearance. "The woman saw that the tree was . . . to be desired to make one wise" (Genesis 3:6). And along with the first man's and woman's giving in to that desire, the natural awareness of God's presence was lost; it would now have to be practiced. Human beings began to experience shame, and competition arose in relationships. The original harmony was disrupted and the balance was destroyed.

Though we do not have the ability to definitively heal the consequences of original sin, we are able to catch glimmers of the divine, original intention for harmony and balance among God, ourselves, and others. This is exactly what acts of penance and asceticism provide for us.

Not simply a way to communicate with God, prayer also makes us prayerful. It helps us to grow in sensitivity to and awareness of the divine presence that pervades all of life. And so it helps us to experience again what was once a natural part of the human condition, when God could be heard walking in the evening breeze.

Fasting keeps us in touch with ourselves and the physical way we get trapped in a shameful cycle of obsession with self-concern, self-image, self-gratification, and self-preservation. Though traditionally practiced with regard to food and drink, fasting can also be applied to Internet sites, television shows, shopping, exercising, e-mails, and other forms of distraction and entertainment. Regular fasting helps to keep the false self in check.

Thus it is written, "The first man, Adam, became a living being"; the last Adam became a life-giving spirit. But it is not the spiritual that is first, but the physical, and then the spiritual. The first man was from the earth, a man of dust; the second man is from heaven. As was the man of dust, so are those who are of the dust; and as is the man of heaven, so are those who

Almsgiving promotes the interdependence with others that God wove within the very fabric of human life. Sharing our financial treasures with others builds a bridge between us and those who have fewer resources and opportunities than we do. Sharing our time and our talents gives us the opportunity to celebrate our innate gifts and to build community. In a real way, this practice helps us to overcome the competitive stance many of us have toward others.

As we submit to the Spirit's transformative process and become little Christs, we also become a new creation (see 2 Corinthians 5:17). Part are of heaven. Just as we have borne the image of the man of dust, we will also bear the image of the man of heaven.

(1 Corinthians 15:45-49)

of our newness, discovered through the traditional practices of prayer, fasting, and almsgiving, is experiencing the fullness of life that Christ, "the last Adam," now enjoys and that God intended for us from the very first day of creation.

■ PRACTICE

Consider your upcoming week and commit to a day of soul training. Before choosing between prayer, fasting, or almsgiving, ask yourself: Do I need to strengthen my awareness of God's presence through prayer, challenge my obsession with the concerns of the false self through fasting, or reinforce my connection with others through almsgiving? Choose just one of the three practices for this day. At the end of the day, reflect upon your experience, perhaps journal about it, and then commit to another session of soul training next week.

■ GO DEEPER

Adalbert de Vogüé, *To Love Fasting: The Monastic Experience* (Petersham, MA: St. Bede's Publications, 1989).

Albert Haase, OFM, *Lenten Penance: Getting Back on Track,* http://www.americancatholic.org/messenger/feb1997/feature1.asp.

Kevin Perrotta, *Prayer, Fasting and Almsgiving: Spiritual Practices That Draw Us Closer to God* (Frederick, MD: Word Among Us Press, 2012).

Donald Spoto, *In Silence: Why We Pray* (New York: Penguin Compass, 2004).

A Prayer at the Hearth of the Heart

■

Catching fire and becoming flame require more than the spark of the Spirit and our well-chosen kindling. They also demand an ongoing perseverance and long-term patience forged from the awareness that God fervently desires to see us blaze with godly enthusiasm. We commit to and continue this spiritual transformation by praying these words each and every day:

O Loving God,
The fiery ardor of your enthusiasm to be in a relationship with me
crackles in every event, person, insight, and longing you send along
    my way.
They are sparks thrown upon the kindling in my hearth.

Ignite my heart with your living flame of love.

O Selfless Jesus,
your soul raged with the desire to set this world ablaze
with the love, mercy, and compassion of your Abba.

Stoke my flame with the wisdom of the gospel
so that I might burn with the same fervor that fueled your life.

O Empowering Spirit,

you are the flint and fuel of God's love that enlightens my vision to
  see those who are in need

and impassions my heart to glow with godly enthusiasm for the
  treasures of heaven.

Transform me into a little Christ willing to die for love of his love,

he who was so ardent as to die for love of my love.

Amen.

Acknowledgments

∎

I am grateful to the hundreds of people who have attended my workshops on prayer and the spiritual life as well as to the listeners of Relevant Radio's *Spirit and Life*, cohosted by my sister, Bridget, osu, and me. Their enthusiasm for these ideas motivated me to write this book and develop its DVD series.

I was blessed with the wise and experienced advice of three seasoned editors. LaVonne Neff noted some structural problems and offered some suggestions that strengthened my presentation. She introduced me to Evelyn Bence, who graciously and meticulously rendered my gobbledygook into readable English; Evelyn's attention to detail was second to none. Jon Sweeney of Paraclete Press showed me how to render a preacher's ideas onto paper; his comments proved invaluable.

Special thanks to Bob Edmonson, who was a gracious tour guide when I visited the Community of Jesus to film the DVD series for this book.

Notes

■

1   John of the Cross, *Dark Night of the Soul,* Book 2, chapter 10.

2   M. Robert Mulholland's classic definition of spiritual formation is "the process of being conformed to the image of Christ for the sake of others." See M. Robert Mulholland, Jr., *Invitation to a Journey: A Road Map for Spiritual Formation* (Downers Grove, IL: InterVarsity Press, 1993), 15.

3   Rev. Francois Jamart, OCD, *Complete Spiritual Doctrine of St. Therese of Lisieux* (New York: Alba House, 1961), 16.

4   Augustine, *Sermo* 117.3.5.

5   Teresa of Avila, *Life*, chapter 8:5. The paraphrase is my own.

6   James Finley, *Merton's Palace of Nowhere* (Notre Dame, IN: Ave Maria Press, 1978), 114.

7   *Collected Works of G. K. Chesterton, Volume X: Collected Poetry: Part 1*, edited by Aidan Mackey (San Francisco: Ignatius Press, 1994), 43.

8   Donna Wilkinson, *The Only 127 Things You Need: A Guide to Life's Essentials* (New York: Tarcher, 2008), 347.

9   Augustine, *Enarrationes in psalmos* 105.

10 Angela of Foligno, *Memorial* 55.

11 Meister Eckhart, "Talks of Instruction," 22.

12 Dennis Hamm, SJ, "Rummaging for God: Praying Backwards through Your Day," *America Magazine,* May 14, 1994.

13 Brother Lawrence of the Resurrection, *The Practice of the Presence of God. Spiritual Maxims,* chapter 6, paragraph 31.

14 Saint Clare of Assisi, "Second Letter to Blessed Agnes of Prague," 20.

15   Douglas J. Leonhardt, sj, "Gospel Contemplation," in *Finding God in All Things: A Marquette Prayer Book* (Milwaukee, WI: Marquette University Press, 2009).

16   Teresa of Avila, *Way of Perfection*, chapters 21, 27; 29:6, 31:3, 13.

17   Brian Kolodiejchuk, mc, ed., Mother Teresa, *Come Be My Light: The Private Writings of the "Saint of Calcutta"* (New York: Doubleday, 2007), 210.

18   Cathy Wright, lsj, *Charles de Foucauld: Journey of the Spirit* (Boston: Pauline Books & Media, 2005), 78.

19   Henri Nouwen, *The Way of the Heart: The Spirituality of the Desert Fathers and Mothers* (New York: HarperOne, 1981), 27.

20   Paraphrase of Francis of Assisi, Admonition 19:2.

21   Nouwen, *The Way of the Heart*, 25.

22   Abraham Joshua Heschel, *The Sabbath: Its Meaning for Modern Man* (New York: Noonday Press, 1975), 18.

ABOUT PARACLETE PRESS

Who We Are

Paraclete Press is a publisher of books, recordings, and DVDs on Christian spirituality. Our publishing represents a full expression of Christian belief and practice—from Catholic to Evangelical, from Protestant to Orthodox.

We are the publishing arm of the Community of Jesus, an ecumenical monastic community in the Benedictine tradition. As such, we are uniquely positioned in the marketplace without connection to a large corporation and with informal relationships to many branches and denominations of faith.

What We Are Doing

Books   Paraclete publishes books that show the richness and depth of what it means to be Christian. Although Benedictine spirituality is at the heart of all that we do, we publish books that reflect the Christian experience across many cultures, time periods, and houses of worship. We publish books that nourish the vibrant life of the church and its people—books about spiritual practice, formation, history, ideas, and customs.

We have several different series, including the best-selling Paraclete Essentials and Paraclete Giants series of classic texts in contemporary English; Voices from the Monastery—men and women monastics writing about living a spiritual life today; award-winning poetry; best-selling gift books for children on the occasions of baptism and first communion; and the Active Prayer Series that brings creativity and liveliness to any life of prayer.

Recordings   From Gregorian chant to contemporary American choral works, our music recordings celebrate sacred choral music through the centuries. Paraclete distributes the recordings of the internationally acclaimed choir Gloriæ Dei Cantores, praised for their "rapt and fathomless spiritual intensity" by *American Record Guide,* and the Gloriæ Dei Cantores Schola, which specializes in the study and performance of Gregorian chant. Paraclete is also the exclusive North American distributor of the recordings of the Monastic Choir of St. Peter's Abbey in Solesmes, France, long considered to be a leading authority on Gregorian chant.

Videos   Our videos offer spiritual help, healing, and biblical guidance for life issues: grief and loss, marriage, forgiveness, anger management, facing death, and spiritual formation.

Learn more about us at our website:

www.paracletepress.com,

or call us toll-free at 1-800-451-5006.

SCAN
TO
READ
MORE

You may also be interested in . . .

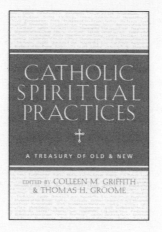

Catholic Spiritual Practices

Growing in faith is all about practice.

This collection by today's most respected Catholic writers offers
a compendium of these practices, traditional and contemporary,
that can enable us to sustain and grow a vibrant spiritual life. This
must-have volume will quickly become a trusted companion for
an entire lifetime of engagement with the beauty and richness of
the Catholic faith.

ISBN: 978-1-61261-246-1 | Hardcover | $18.99